WINNING MONOLOGS
for
YOUNG ACTORS

*65 honest-to-life characterizations
to delight young actors and audiences
of all ages*

PEG KEHRET

MERIWETHER PUBLISHING LTD.
COLORADO SPRINGS, COLORADO

Meriwether Publishing Ltd., Publisher
P.O. Box 7710
Colorado Springs, CO 80933

Cover & Inside Design: Michelle Z. Gallardo
Executive Editor: Arthur L. Zapel
Manuscript Editor: Kathy Pijanowski

© Copyright MCMLXXXVI Meriwether Publishing Ltd.
Printed in the United States of America
First Edition

Library of Congress Cataloging-in-Publication Data

Kehret, Peg.
Winning monologs for young actors.

Summary: A collection of sixty-five monologues
providing young performers with a variety of audition
pieces reflecting situations both serious and comic.
1. Monologues — Juvenile literature. 2. Acting —
Auditions — Juvenile literature. [1. Monologues.
2. Acting — Auditions] I. Title.
PN2080.K36 1987   812'.54   86-61109
ISBN 0-916260-38-0

9   10   11   12   02   01   00   99   98

For my son, Bob C. Kehret,
who taught me to love baseball, beards and little boys

PREFACE

When I was 14 years old, I had my first part in a play. It was a one-act comedy, performed in my school auditorium, and I played the role of an elderly hillbilly. We gave just one performance, but that single performance had a profound effect on me.

I remember standing backstage, waiting for the curtain to open. My mother was in the audience; butterflies were in my stomach. When a burst of laughter followed my first line, the butterflies instantly disappeared.

Afterwards — oh, I do remember afterwards — all the kids talked about how funny I was as the old hillbilly, and my teacher told me I'd done a good job, and my mother said she wished my father could have been there. I was giddy with success; I was addicted to live theatre.

In the years after that debut, I tried out for many roles in many plays. When I got cast, I was ecstatic. When I didn't, I worked backstage and found that the production end of theatre is fun, too.

Eventually, I discovered that I like writing plays even more than I like acting in them, and I went on to a career as a professional writer. Now I sit in darkened theatres and wait for the curtain to go up on plays I've written. Each time, I feel the same tingling of anticipation and nervousness that I felt so long ago in the school auditorium. Will the pace be right? Will everyone remember his lines? Will the audience laugh and cry in the appropriate places? Each performance is different, even if the same cast has done the show many times before. That's part of the fun of live theatre: we start fresh every day.

These audition pieces are written for young people who are discovering the joys of being on stage. I've been asked if the scenes are autobiographical. The answer is no — and yes. The monologs in this book are fiction, but to some extent, everything I write is autobiographical. All of my plays, as well as my books and the pieces I do for magazines, reflect who I am and what I am.

It is my hope that these monologs will help you, the emerging actor or actress, to discover who and what you are, and then to go even further. By using this material to audition, may you reveal your special talent to others and use it as your stepping stone to a lifelong association with the theatre.

Break a leg.

Peg Kehret

INTRODUCTION

As a creative drama teacher, how often do you find material that will interest young actors? As a parent, how often do you find material that is suitable for your child actor? As a young actor, how often do you find monologs that really reflect your feelings and experiences?

I feel quite certain that the answer to these questions will be a resounding "no, never, not once." Most of us — teachers, parents and actors — have always had to resort to adapting adult roles in plays to find audition material for young people.

Well, those days are over! Peg Kehret has written 65 "winning monologs" for boys and girls. And indeed they are *winning,* for each one is designed to speak directly to the young actor and echo his or her own personal experience. Those actors no longer have to resort to playing Willie Loman or Blanche DuBois for auditions. The monologs are also wonderful acting exercises for drama classes, incidentally.

Try out these pieces. I know you will be as relieved as I am to find this lovely book.

Libby Appel
Dean and Artistic Director
Theatre School
California Institute of the Arts

CONTENTS

Part Three:
MONOLOGS FOR BOYS OR GIRLS

Part One:

MONOLOGS FOR GIRLS

#1

They'll Be Sorry
When I'm Dead

It's awfully stuffy up here in the attic. I should have brought a pillow and something to read.

I wonder if they've missed me yet. Probably not. I haven't heard anyone calling. They haven't even noticed that I'm gone. Well, they'll be sorry when I'm dead. Will they ever be sorry then! They'll think back to all the times they were mean to me and they'll wish they could do it differently. But it'll be too late then.

I've thought about hiding in the attic before, but this is the first time I've ever done it. It'll be the last time, too, because I plan to stay right here until I die. I'm never going down there again. I wonder how long it will be before they find me. Maybe the police will bring dogs to sniff out my body. The police will ask when I was last seen and nobody will know for sure. That'll make them feel guilty.

I hope they have a funeral for me. All my friends could come and cry and bring flowers and tell my family what a wonderful person I was and they'll say, *We know, we know. We never appreciated her, and now it's too late.*

It wasn't my fault that I got tar all over my new white coat. All I did was wear it to school, and in order to get to school I had to walk across the street, and I couldn't help it that the city decided to put fresh tar on the street today. I was afraid of getting tar on my shoes, so I ran across the street instead of walking. How was I supposed to know that this would make the tar fly up off my feet and get all over the back of my new white coat? I don't think it's fair that I got punished for something I couldn't help, just because Mom told me not to wear the coat to school. Well, she'll be sorry when I'm dead. She'll cry and be lonesome for me. I just hope she doesn't give my coat to Suzie.

Suzie's such a spoiled baby. She always gets her way, just because she's the youngest. I bet if Suzie had got tar on her new coat, Mom would have said, "Oh, that's all right. She didn't know any better." Suzie gets away with murder because she never knows any better.

My parents are so unfair! I made a bet with Suzie and I won, and then they wouldn't let me keep the money. It was an honest bet, too. We were doing the dishes and I was washing and Suzie was drying and I bet her twenty-five cents that I would finish before she did. I won, naturally, and she had to give me the twenty-five cents. The next night we made the bet again, and since Suzie never wants to wash, only dry, I won that night, too. The third time I won, Suzie started crying, the big baby, and then Mom wanted to know what was wrong and when Suzie told her, Mom made me give the seventy-five cents back. Talk about unfair! A bet's a bet, and if Suzie is too stupid to figure out that she can't ever finish drying before I finish washing, that's her problem.

I smell popcorn. I can't believe it! I am a missing person, whereabouts unknown, and they're all down there eating popcorn. They haven't even missed me. Boy, will they ever be sorry when I'm dead.

I suppose Suzie will eat my share of the popcorn. From now on, she'll probably always get my share of everything. When Mom makes chocolate frosting, Suzie'll get to lick the pan all by herself, and she'll always get the wishbone and . . .

Maybe I *won't* stay up here 'til I die.

#2

Mr. Bartholomew

Mr. Bartholomew was the most beautiful cat in the world. In the universe! He was mostly black, with three white feet and a white bib. There was also a tiny bit of white on the tip of his tail, but unless you were looking close, you'd never notice. He had a deep, rumbling purr that came from far down in his chest and made the white bib vibrate.

I got Mr. Bartholomew when I was three years old. He used to let me dress him up in doll's clothes and push him around in the doll buggy. I put bonnets on him and little dresses and he didn't seem to mind at all. The only thing he didn't like was booties. When I put booties on his feet, he'd bite and claw 'til he got them off, so I quit doing it. Once when I was pushing Mr. Bartholomew in the buggy, a dog started barking at us and Mr. Bartholomew jumped out of the buggy and ran up a tree. He looked pretty funny sitting up there in that oak tree wearing a lavender dress with lace on the collar. Mrs. Downing, who used to live down the street from us and whose oak tree Mr. Bartholomew climbed, came out and took a picture of him. I still have it in my Save Box.

Besides being beautiful, Mr. Bartholomew was intelligent. Once, I counted, and he had a vocabulary of fourteen words. That is, he recognized fourteen different words and knew what they meant. Things like *no* and *down* and *good kitty*. He knew his name, of course, and he also recognized the sound of the can opener, but I didn't count that as a word.

Secretly, I always expected Mr. Bartholomew to set a record for longevity. Since he was the prettiest cat I'd ever seen and the smartest, I thought he would probably be the oldest, too. My brother, Randy, who goes to college, talked to me one time about what we would do if Mr. Bartholomew got very sick and couldn't have fun anymore. I agreed that I would never want him to be in pain and if the doctor said Mr. Bartholomew couldn't get well, we would have him put to sleep. I didn't like talking about it or even thinking about it, but at the same time, I felt sort of protective and heroic, knowing I would be able to keep my furry friend from suffering.

Mr. Bartholomew didn't set the record for old cats after all. As smart as he was, he never learned to stop and look before he crossed the street, and one summer night, he didn't make it.

Randy found him. He came home to get a box to put Mr. Bartholomew in and I cried when he told me. I ran out of the house, out to the street, with Randy running after me, telling me not to look. I looked anyway and then I wished I hadn't.

We buried him in the back yard, under the apple tree that he always used to sharpen his claws on. In the spring, I sit there in the grass. I lean my back against the tree trunk and look up at the apple blossoms and wish Mr. Bartholomew could sit on my lap again, and purr.

#3

The Fire Drill

There was a fire drill at my school yesterday. According to the fire marshal, everyone is supposed to vacate the building in two minutes and thirty-seven seconds, or less. I don't know where he came up with that figure, but it is totally unrealistic. The only way everyone in the school could get outside in that amount of time is if we all jumped out the windows.

I was in my math class when the fire alarm rang. Since this was the first fire drill of the season, I wasn't sure what it was. They ring one kind of bell for an earthquake drill and a different kind of bell for a fire drill. If it's an earthquake drill, we're supposed to duck and take cover. If it's a fire drill, we're supposed to go outside. Nobody could remember which was which, so when the alarm sounded, the first thing we did was ask each other if that was the fire drill alarm or the earthquake drill alarm. We were so busy asking each other and saying we didn't know that it was about half a minute before anyone noticed that our teacher was telling us it was a fire alarm and to get outside.

My seat in math class is next to the window. I remembered that the people next to the windows are supposed to do something during a fire drill but I couldn't remember what. Was I supposed to close the window so the fresh air couldn't get in and feed the flames? Or was I supposed to open the window so the pressure of hot air wouldn't cause it to shatter? I tried it both ways and debated a few seconds about each one. In the end, I left it slightly ajar.

When the window question was decided, I had to gather up all my books. I couldn't leave them behind. What if they got lost? What if it really was a fire and they burned up? I'd spent two hours the night before decorating my paper book covers. I used colored pens and wrote "I Love Justin" fourteen different ways. I couldn't just rush out of the room and leave my books behind.

As soon as I had all my books, I went out in the hall to look for Marybeth and Lisa. We had agreed that we would meet as soon as fourth-period class was over because Marybeth had some critical news to tell us and it could not wait until lunch period. I suspected it had to do with Mark Hanover, the guy Marybeth likes, and if I didn't find out what it was after fourth period, I wouldn't see her again until lunch, and by then she'd have told Lisa and Lisa would tell everyone else and I'd be the last to know, which wouldn't be right at all, since I am one of Marybeth's closest friends.

So I left my math room and went to where I was supposed to meet Lisa and Marybeth. Lisa was already there and as soon as Marybeth arrived, we went to my locker. I had to stop at my locker because I'd left my purse in it and I couldn't possibly leave the building without my purse. My purse contains every single item of importance to my existence and I'd sooner die in the fire than lose it.

After I got my purse, Lisa had to stop at her locker and get *her* purse. By then, the building was almost empty, so it was the perfect time for Marybeth to tell us her news without anyone else hearing. The news *was* critical! Mark Hanover had said *hi* to her in the hall that morning and she said *hi* back — so no wonder she was anxious to tell us about it. We were still exclaiming about Marybeth's good fortune when one of the teachers yelled at us to hurry up and get outside.

We got out to the east parking lot, where we were supposed to go, and checked in with the monitor. Then we had to listen to a big lecture about how it took ten minutes and fifty-three seconds to evacuate the building, which was not acceptable, and next time we have a fire alarm, we're supposed to leave the building *immediately.*

I don't know what he was so cross about. It should have been obvious that we had already hurried as fast as we could.

#4

Missing Mandy

Last year on the first day of school, Mandy and I walked together. I miss Mandy a lot. It might not be so bad if I could write to her and get letters back from her, but to have her just leave like she did and not know where she went — well, that part's hard.

I always wonder what would have happened if I'd told sooner. Would she still have moved away and not let anyone know where?

Last year when school started, I didn't know anything about Mandy's trouble. She never told anyone, not even me. I thought she always wore long-sleeved shirts because she liked them. I didn't know she wanted to cover up the bruises.

One day Mandy came to school with her hand bandaged. She'd burned it baking cookies. That day our teacher, Mrs. Swenson, asked me to stay after school. When we were alone, she asked me if I thought Mandy had really burned herself baking cookies. I told her Mandy wouldn't pretend to be burned if she wasn't.

Mrs. Swenson said she was sure the burn was real, but she wasn't convinced it was accidental. I didn't know what she meant.

And then one night Mandy was supposed to come over to my house so we could do our homework together, and she didn't come. When I went to her house to get her, I could hear her crying. What's worse, I heard *why* she was crying. I stood there on Mandy's front porch in the dark and I could hear her daddy beating on her something fierce. I got all sick-feeling inside and I didn't know what to do.

Finally, I pounded, hard, on Mandy's door and pretty soon her daddy opened the door, and when I saw him standing there, looking down at me with the sweat standing out in little droplets on his upper lip, I couldn't say anything. I just stood there with my knees shaking and stared at him. He told me Mandy wasn't feeling well and for me to go on home.

I did. I sat on my bed in the dark, but I couldn't stop shaking, even after I crawled under the covers and put my pillow over my head.

I stayed home from school the next day. I told Mama I felt sick and that was the truth. Mama asked me what was wrong, but I couldn't tell her. Would things have turned out different if I had?

When I went back to school, Mandy was there and neither of us said anything about that night. A few weeks later, Mandy showed up with a cast on her arm. She said she'd fallen down her basement steps, but there was a odd, faraway look in her eye when she told me.

That afternoon I stayed after school and told Mrs. Swenson about standing on Mandy's porch and hearing her daddy whomp on her. Mrs. Swenson kept nodding at me, as if she wasn't at all surprised, and then she said I'd done right to tell her.

I don't know if it was right or not. A police car stopped at Mandy's house that afternoon, but there was nobody home, and when the police went back the next day, Mandy was gone. She and her daddy must have moved out in the night because nobody saw them leave and nobody knows where they went.

Mrs. Swenson isn't my teacher anymore, and this year I walk to school alone. I hope Mandy isn't walking alone. Wherever she is, I hope she has a friend to talk with. Most of all, I hope she's wearing a shirt with short sleeves.

#5

Beauty for Sale

Shawna, wait until you see what I have. We are going to make some unbelievable changes in our bodies! A month from now, we'll look in the mirror and we won't know who we're seeing. We're going to be gorgeous, my friend. Not just gorgeous. We're also going to be sexy, smart and happy. And all because I had the good sense to buy this magazine and read the ads. We'll do a total make-over. We'll change our lives!

Listen to this. *(She reads.)* "Make your dingy teeth look radiantly white! Do you have dull, discolored, unattractive teeth? Now you can cover stains. Cover blemishes. Have a sparkling movie-star smile in just ten days or your money back."

Isn't that great? We just brush this gunk on our teeth and in ten days, we sparkle! What could be easier?

Or, here's another one. "Add 3½ inches to your bustline in only two short weeks. Amazing new discovery! Apply this miracle cream to your bust for a few minutes each day and see your bustline grow, right before your eyes."

Imagine, Shawna! If we both add 3½ inches, let's see . . . twenty-nine plus 3½ . . . we'll be knockouts!

Are you embarrassed by ugly stretch marks? You're not? Neither am I. Maybe we'll skip that one and go right on to The Diet that Will Let Us Flush Ourselves Down the Drain. These miracle pills are going to take the excess water out of our thighs, our rear ends and our stomachs. We don't even have to diet, but we'll lose up to five pounds the very first day.

Oh, and look at this ad. Here's a special formula which will give us beautiful, curly hair without a permanent. We just shampoo it in and we get thick, soft, luxurious curls.

And you haven't heard the best news of all. Not only are we going to gain 3½ inches up front, we are going to have the greatest behinds ever known. *(Reads.)* "Do you have a flat, shapeless fanny?

Do you have Secretary Spread? A sagging butt? No matter what your backside problem might be, The Beautiful Bottom Plan will eliminate the trouble. No more bouncing buns! No more Jello jiggle!'

Shawna, we are going to be irresistible, coming and going.

What do you mean, you can't afford all this? It's only $8.95 for the curly hair and thirteen dollars for the bustline cream. Heck, that's just $3.71 per inch. Wouldn't it be worth $3.71 an inch? And your beautiful bottom is going to set you back a mere $7.50.

I know it adds up, but think how you'll look. And the money won't be any problem; the magazine makes sure of that. It says right here, "Your debt problems are over."

Shawna, wait! I haven't told you about the Painless Pimple Popper that lets you zap your zits while you sleep!

Shawna? Well, if she doesn't want to be beautiful, that's her problem. I think I'll start with the Elegant Eyelash Extender.

#6

Wedding Woes

It is absolute chaos at my house. You would think that my sister Elaine's engagement was the major event of this century. What's the big deal? People get married every day of the year and I don't notice any other household being thrown into total bedlam.

I can't even make a telephone call. Elaine hogs the phone constantly, asking someone to pour the punch, asking someone else to cut the cake. And the minute Elaine hangs up, my mother takes over. She has practically worn out the Yellow Pages trying to find inexpensive dripless candles. My father said she should just go buy the candles she found and never mind the cost. Actually, he said, "Go buy the damn candles and to hell with the cost," but I get in trouble when I talk like he does. Mom just looked at him and kept on dialing. She's determined to find a bargain, if she can.

I don't know what difference it makes how much the candles cost. The rest of the wedding is so expensive, we're going to have to file for bankruptcy anyway, so what's a couple dozen candles added to the total? The whole thing makes me sick. Think of the neat vacation we could take with all that money. But no, we're spending it all on dumb stuff like white chrysanthemums and renting a silver punch bowl. Who cares whether the punch bowl is silver or Tupperware, as long as the punch tastes good?

I probably won't even go to the stupid wedding. By then I'll be so tired of hearing about it, I'll fall asleep in my pew anyway. I think I'll stay home that day and watch TV. Or call my friends. That's what I'll do. I'll stay home and call Susan and for once we'll be able to talk without Elaine telling me to hurry up and get off the phone because she needs to use it.

If you ask me, the whole wedding is a waste of time. Why don't they just go off and get married and be done with it? If *I* ever get married, you can bet I'll elope. I wouldn't go through all this mess for anything. And I sure wouldn't expect everyone in my whole family to stop everything else in their lives just so I could plan a big, fancy wedding.

Right at this moment, nobody in this entire family can talk about anything except Elaine's wedding. It's disgusting. I could flunk out of school tomorrow and they wouldn't even notice. The only one who pays any attention to me is Snooper, and all he does is wag his tail.

To tell you the truth, I think big weddings are so stupid that they should not be legal. We should pass a law that if people want to get married, they have twenty-four hours to either do it or forget it.

What did you say, Elaine? Were you talking to me? You do? *Me?* You want *me* to be a bridesmaid and wear a long dress and flowers in my hair and stand up in front with you? No kidding? Well, sure, I'd like to do it. I'd love to do it! Wow! Wait 'til I tell Susan I'm going to be a bridesmaid!

#7

I Thought Ellen
Was My Friend

I thought Ellen was my friend. We had so much fun together. We talked for hours at a time, about all different things, and we laughed a lot and shared our secrets. She was like a sister and I even told her about the crush I've had forever on Rob Schuman, who lives next door to me. I'd never told anyone about Rob before, but I felt safe telling Ellen because I thought we'd be friends forever.

I was wrong.

A few months ago, Ellen and I tried out for the school play. She got a part and I didn't. I didn't feel too bad. I volunteered to help with props and I spent hours finding all the things we needed and making arrangements to borrow them. I went to all the rehearsals, too, even though the props people weren't required to attend until the last week. It was fun to go and besides, Rob Schuman was in the cast.

One night I went early because it was Rob's birthday and I had a card for him. I planned to leave it backstage, where he would find it.

As I arrived, I heard Ellen calling to the other girls to come because she was ready to take the cake to the boys' dressing room. I hurried backstage and was astounded to see Ellen lighting the candles on a big chocolate cake that said *Happy Birthday, Rob.* All the girls in the cast were gathering around her and when I joined them, Ellen looked surprised.

Then she said, "This party is just for the *cast,*" and she picked up the cake and marched down the hall to where Rob and the other guys were dressing. I heard her start singing the Happy Birthday song when she reached the dressing room door.

I didn't leave Rob's card backstage. I didn't even stay for the rehearsal. I left the school and walked home, trying not to cry.

At first I was angry. I'd worked as hard on the play as anyone in the cast; why should I be excluded from the party? I was jealous, too, but that didn't last long, because I knew Rob wasn't my boyfriend in the first place, so Ellen couldn't steal him away from me.

In the end, I just felt sad. Ellen was not my friend, after all.

#8

The Stepsister Speaks Out

It isn't easy being the ugly stepsister. Everybody always feels so sorry for poor little Cinderella, but what about me? I deserve a little sympathy, too. Does *my* fairy godmother ever turn up with a magic wand? Does the prince ever dance with me at the ball? Not on your life. The best I can ever hope for with my pumpkins is a decent piece of pie. And as for the rats, well, rats are rats, with their sneaky eyes and skinny tails, nibbling and gnawing at the garbage. I never saw one yet who turned into a coachman.

If you ask me, that Cinderella is weird. Certainly, she isn't normal. Besides the fact that she has naturally curly hair and wears size 4½ shoes, she is so good-natured that it's downright sickening. If you had to dust and sweep and clean all day long, would you go around singing to the birds? Of course you wouldn't. No sensible person would.

A lot of people think I'm jealous of her. Maybe I am. And with good reason. I subsisted on seven hundred calories a day for three whole weeks before the ball. I did my leg-lift exercises faithfully. I got a perm and a facial and a manicure. I even bought a new gown. Blue velvet. Designer label. I mean, I was *ready*. *Princey*, I thought to myself, *here I come!*

And what happens? Little Cindy, who has never seen the inside of a health club in her life and who doesn't know the caloric difference between a carrot stick and a chocolate eclair, whips together a dress out of some old curtains from K-Mart, waltzes off to the ball and snags the prince.

It isn't fair! It really isn't fair!

#9

First Date

I suppose every girl dreams about what it will be like when she goes on her first date. I know I did. For months — no, make that *years* — before I ever had a real date, I daydreamed about how it would be. I don't mean vague daydreams, like, "some guy will ask me to go out with him," I mean specific daydreams, like "Kurt Andrews will call me and when I say *hello,* he'll say, *You are the most beautiful girl I've ever seen and I hope you'll do me the honor of attending the Harvest Dance with me.*"

I imagined what would happen on the night of the dance too. Kurt would bring me flowers — not ordinary flowers — something unusual, something exquisite. A bouquet of tiger lilies, perhaps, or a nosegay of violets and baby orchids. He'd help me with my coat and open the door of his Porsche for me and while we drove to the dance, we'd have a scintillating conversation on a variety of topics.

I could tell you what I thought would happen at the dance, too, but perhaps you'd rather hear what *really* happened on my first date. To begin with, it wasn't Kurt Andrews who called, it was Herbert McFish. This was something of a surprise, since I avoid Herbert McFish whenever possible.

He said, "This is Herbert. Ya wanna go-to-the-movies Friday night?"

I said, "You mean, with you?" and he said, "A'course I mean with me, stupid, why-do-ya think I'm callin' ya up?"

At that point, I had to make a decision. Did I want to have the experience of going on a real date badly enough to say *yes* to Herbert? To be bluntly honest, did I want to have the experience of calling all my girlfriends and telling them I had a date badly enough to let the date be with Herbert?

I did. He said he'd pick me up at 6:45. That gave me two days to decide what to wear. My good dress and heels? My navy

lacks and grey blazer? A sweater and skirt with flats? In the end,
wore the slacks and blazer. Herbert wore jeans and a sweatshirt
hat said "Hot Tricks" on the front.

His father drove us because Herbert flunked the written
art of the driver's test and didn't have his license yet. Not only
lid his father drive us, his mother rode along. She asked me so
nany questions that Herbert and I had no time for scintillating
onversation.

The movie was terrible, a senseless plot with lots of blood
and violence. I went to the rest room twice, just so I wouldn't have
o watch.

In my daydreams, the dance was always followed by a late
andlelight supper, with soft music in the background. I was
ealistic enough not to expect a candlelight supper after a movie
vith Herbert, but I did think we might go somewhere for a hamburger
r a hot fudge sundae. I would have been happy with McDonalds,
ust so I could tell my friends we went out to eat after the movie.

But when we came out of the theatre, there were Mr. and
Mrs. McFish, double-parked in front, watching for us. Mrs.
McFish got out of the car and waved, and shouted, "Herbie! Over
ere!" She had her hair in rollers. I devoutly prayed that no one
knew could see me.

When the ride home was mercifully over, Herbert walked
o the door with me. I lied and told him I'd had a wonderful time.

In my daydreams, Kurt Andrews always kissed me good
light. Herbert couldn't — not with his parents watching us. I
vas glad about that. There are some experiences I simply don't
vant, not even if I get to tell my friends.

#10

Tammi's Brother Is Dead

Tammi's little brother is dead. Billy. I can't believe it! How can Billy be dead when he is only nine years old?

Tammi's family went on a vacation, a camping trip in the mountains. Billy apparently tried to wade across a river and slipped and fell and hit his head on a rock. They aren't sure if the rock killed him or if he drowned. It doesn't matter. Dead is dead, no matter how it happened.

Billy was the same age as my brother, Mark. Tammi and I used to complain to each other about what pests they were, always tagging around after us and listening to our conversations. They were always asking us to take them over to the shopping mall for a hot fudge sundae because they weren't allowed to go alone. A couple of times when Tammi and I went to the movies on Saturday afternoons, we had to take Billy and Mark with us, and we always made them sit on the other side of the theatre, away from us.

Tammi called me this morning and told me. When I answered the phone, I was surprised to hear from her because she wasn't supposed to get back from the camping trip until next Sunday. Then she told me Billy is dead and I didn't know what to say. I was too shocked to respond. Tammi sounded scared, as if everything had happened too fast and she didn't know yet how she was going to deal with it.

This afternoon I bought some flowers and took them to Tammi's house and we sat in her room for a long time and talked about Billy and how, even when we said our brothers were a pain in the butt, we really didn't mean it.

I could tell Tammi was feeling guilty about every unkind thing she'd ever said or done to Billy so I tried to remember some of the times when she was really nice to him. I reminded her of how she stood outside the supermarket with him one whole Saturday because Billy had to sell tickets to the Cub Scout car wash and he

as too timid to do it alone. I talked about the time Billy wanted
to build a snow fort in the back yard and we helped him do it even
though our hands were half-frozen by the time we finished.

Tammi didn't cry. I could tell from her red eyes that she'd
been crying before I came, but she just sat on her bed and talked
about Billy, as if he might walk in at any moment, the way he
used to, and ask to borrow her bicycle.

When I got back home, I shut myself in my room for a long
time. I buried my head in my pillow and wept. I cried for Billy,
who would not get to be an Eagle Scout like he planned. I cried
for Tammi because her brother was gone and would never return.
And I cried for myself because I knew the kind of tragedy which
struck Tammi's family could happen to anyone. Even to me. For
the first time in my life, I felt vulnerable.

Eventually, the tears stopped and I washed my face and
combed my hair. Then I went downstairs and looked for Mark.
When I found him, I asked him if he'd like to go get a hot fudge
sundae. My treat.

#11

The Bargain

Last winter I learned to paint. I'm not particularly artisti but my mother wanted to take a class called Tole Painting and th craft shop which offered the classes had a two-for-the-price-of-on special, which meant two people could take the class but on one of them had to pay. My mother can't pass up a bargain. Non of her friends wanted to do Tole Painting, so I was drafted.

"It'll be fun," she told me. "You'll learn to appreciate colc and form. You'll develop a new skill. And you won't have to do th dishes on Monday nights." Mom can be mighty convincing whe she puts her mind to it.

The class cost thirty dollars and lasted for six weeks. Ever Monday, from seven until nine, we sat at some tables at the bac of the craft shop. Customers kept wandering in and watching us.

The first night, the instructor gave us a list of the supplie we would need and told us to bring them to the next class. Part on of the list was easy: paper towels, a notebook, an apron or old shir to wear. The second part were things we needed to buy: a palett knife, a palette pad, oil or acrylic paints and brushes — one fla one round, one detail and one liner. The instructor pointed ou that all of the necessary supplies were available right there a the craft shop and students received a ten percent discount o all purchases.

Everyone got up and started to select the supplies the needed. I had decided to paint a bouquet of daisies, so I was gettin tubes of yellow, white and green paint when Mom came over an told me that she was going to paint daisies, too, so we would b sharing all our supplies. When I asked why, she pointed to th price on the paint. I gasped. Each little tube was $3.98.

The brushes were even worse. Then we had to pay $4.1 for an eight-ounce can of odorless turpentine, to clean the brushe with. A small plastic container to pour some of the turp into wa nother ninety-eight cents. An old cottage cheese carton would ave worked just fine, but we didn't have one with us.

The total that first night came to $47.61. Our bargain class vas getting pretty expensive.

The second week we had to buy waxless tracing paper so hat we could copy the daisies we were going to paint. We also needed raphite paper, which only came in large rolls. We learned that ve needed black paint to mix with the yellow to get the right shade f green for the daisy leaves, and the small pieces of wood to paint he daisies on were not just scraps of lumber provided by the hop. No, they were called découpage wood and came with a price ag — minus our ten percent discount, of course. It was clear why he shop could afford to let two people take the class for the price f one. Mom and I were sharing supplies, but everyone else in he class was buying individually. The totals were staggering.

By the fourth week, we finished our daisy pictures. They didn't urn out too well, but the instructor said we can't expect perfection n the first try. For my next project, I decided to paint a wooden orse to hang in my room. Small horses were eleven dollars; large orses were twenty-three dollars. Mom said she didn't think I ad room for a large one. She chose to do little wooden pieces of ruit with magnets on the back.

I never did finish the horse. The class ended when I was alf-done and Mom refused to let me sign up for a second session. he finished the fruit magnets at home. She said since we threw way the daisy pictures and the horse wasn't going to get finished, hose magnets cost her ninety-eight dollars plus tax and she asn't going to waste it.

Mom gave the magnets to my Grandma for her birthday nd Grandma was thrilled. She said handmade gifts are best and just goes to prove that you don't need to spend a lot of money o give a really nice present. I looked at Mom and Mom looked t me. Neither of us said a word.

#12

Three-Kleenex Movies

There are many kinds of movies — horror movies, comedies, adventure films, romances. But the kind of movie I like best doesn't have any particular category. I like a movie that makes me cry.

There are degrees of sadness in these movies. Some only make me misty-eyed. In a Misty Movie, I can blink several times and the moisture evaporates or I can pretend to scratch my ear while I wipe away any trace of tears. That way, the person I'm with doesn't suspect that I'm misty-eyed. Misty Movies are usually good but not the kind you want to see more than once or urge all your friends to see.

One step up on the sad-movie success ladder are the Tricklers. In a Trickler Movie, I go just a bit further. The tears will well up and then gradually overflow from one eye and trickle down my cheek. It isn't a steady stream of tears, merely a single trickle and I can adjust my glasses or brush my hair back or use some other excuse to bring my hand to my face and get rid of the tear before anyone notices it.

When I attend a Trickler Movie with my friends, we watch each other out of the corners of our eyes. Everyone wants to see if the other people are crying or not. Probably the Trickler Movie would affect me more profoundly if my attention wasn't partially diverted by watching my friends and knowing they are watching me.

Despite our attempts to appear unmoved in a Trickler Movie, we all agree that the very best movies of all are the Three-Kleenex Movies, where all pretense at controlling our tears is abandoned. In a Three-Kleenex Movie, you have no choice but to wipe your eyes — several times — and blow your nose and let the whole world know you're crying. These are the movies where I watch all the credits at the end, not because I care who did the make-up or ran the camera, but because I need those extra minutes to compose myself so I'm not sobbing as I leave the theatre.

Many of the classic animal films, like *Dumbo* and *Bambi*, e Three-Kleenex Movies, but I've been known to weep and blow er people stories, too.

Three-Kleenex Movies are best seen in a theatre. If you atch them on television or a VCR at home, it just isn't the same. or one thing, there is usually a light on and that inhibits your actions somewhat. Also, because the screen is smaller, the characters n't seem quite as real.

A theatre is an impersonal place, a place where I can cry onymously. I can lose myself in the story and weep for the people the screen. It's a form of cartharsis because I always feel better terwards.

Tears are good for the movie business. Any time I see a ovie that makes me cry, I'm sure to tell all my friends to go to it. ey do the same for me.

Perhaps Hollywood needs a new rating system. Forget e PG and the R and the X categories. If they really want people line up at the ticket window, rate the movie Three-Kleenex. guarantee it'll be a success.

#13

Listening to the Grown-up Ladies Talk

There's a special place in our spare bedroom, right by the heat register, where I can hear the grown-up ladies talk. Nobody else knows about it and I don't plan to tell, either. I just tippy-toe in there, when no one's looking, and lie down on the floor and put my head right close to the register, and I can hear everything they're saying downstairs. It works best in the summertime. In the winter, the furnace keeps coming on and blowing hot air in my face.

Grown-up ladies sure talk funny. For one thing, they talk at the same time as each other. I don't see how they keep track when they're trying to talk and listen all at once. I suppose it's a skill that comes from lots of practice, sort of like patting your head and rubbing your stomach. Sometimes they even play cards *and* talk and listen, all at the same time.

Tonight they talked about the new neighbors, who moved in yesterday. Mama said she'd heard they were both doctors, with money up to the kazoo, and Mrs. Miller said *she'd* heard that they had seven children, all under ten years old, and another on the way, and Mrs. Johnson said, well, if that's the case, it's a good thing they do have plenty of money, and Mama said if they're both doctors, you'd think they would know more about birth control.

Then Mrs. Miller said she saw the movers carry in two pianos and an organ and Mrs. Johnson said maybe they aren't doctors, maybe they're musicians, and Mama said she certainly hopes not because she never met a musician who could afford eight children.

They all agreed it would be nice to welcome the new family, so tomorrow they're going to take dinner over. Mrs. Wilson's making her turkey-rice casserole and Mrs. Johnson's baking her fudge frosting brownies and Mama's going to take cole slaw and a loaf banana bread. I hope she makes double, so there's some for us. They said it would be a nice, neighborly gesture, but I think they also want to find out if the new neighbors are doctors or musicians.

I like it best when the ladies talk about their kids because then I get to listen to what Mama says about me. I love to hear her tell the others what I've been doing. I don't know why that's so interesting, because I already know everything I've done, but that's always the best part — when Mama talks about me. Tonight she told how I'm growing so fast I'm going to need new school clothes again and how I might need braces on my teeth and how I surprised her on her birthday because Grandma taught me to knit and I knitted Mama a scarf. A red scarf, 'cause red's her favorite color. Listening to that part was wonderful. I could tell Mama was proud and that she really likes her scarf and wasn't just pretending because it was from me.

I lay there on the floor, with my head pressed tight against the register, and I just smiled and smiled to myself as I listened to the grown-up ladies talk.

#14

The New Kid

It is the first day of school and I think I'm going to throw up. My parents say I'm just excited and I'll be fine as soon as I get there, but I'm not so sure. I think there's a distinct possibility that I'll lose my breakfast somewhere between my front door and the front steps of Cloverdale Junior High.

I hate going to a new school. I wish we'd never moved. I've changed my clothes three times and I still don't know what I'm going to wear today. How can I decide when I don't know what anyone else is wearing? Back home, I always knew exactly what all my friends were going to wear on the first day of school. I would never have to guess if people were getting all dressed up or if they were wearing jeans.

I would know what to do with my hair, too. What if everyone has perms? What if I'm the only person at Cloverdale Junior High with straight hair? I should have curled it. If I got there and found out I was the only one with curls, I could put my head in the sink and rinse the curls out. No, I couldn't. Someone would see me and think I was retarded.

Everyone will probably stare at me. Then they'll whisper about me behind my back. "Who's the new kid?" they'll say. "Did you see what she's wearing? What a weirdo!"

I'll tell you one thing. If I am the tallest girl in my entire class again this year, I am coming right back home. I don't care if I get kicked out of school for good, I'm not going to be the tallest person. I will run away from home and join a carnival or get a job scrubbing the bathrooms in gas stations before I'll be the tallest girl in my class again.

Last year I was. Even though I scrunched way down whenever possible, I always had to be in the back row for school pictures and if there weren't enough boys to go around when we square-danced in P.E., I always had to dance the boy's part. Well, no more.

managed to live through it last year because I knew everyone and had a lot of friends, but this year I don't know anyone and I'll probably never have a friend again in my whole life. I refuse to be the newest kid and the tallest one, too. They'll think I'm some kind of freak.

Oh, no. It's time to go. And I still have to change my clothes. Now I know how the early martyrs felt when they heard the lions roar. Is there anything in the world more terrible than being a new kid on the first day of school?

#15

Last Chance for the Dance

(Actor enters, carrying a large white dish towel.) Sometimes I really impress myself. Every once in a while, I get a fantastic idea — a really great, creative idea. This *(Holds up dish towel)* is such an idea. This may look like an ordinary dish towel, but it isn't. No, indeed. It is the devious device which is going to save me from being the laughing stock of the entire seventh grade.

Tomorrow night is the Seventh-Grade Dance. It's the first boy/girl dance of my junior-high career and today is the final day to get tickets for it. This means that if anyone is planning to ask anyone else to go to the dance, today is the last day to do the asking.

It is painful for me to admit this, but I do not have a date for the Seventh-Grade Dance, nor is there any potential date in sight. Everyone else is going. Everyone! Even Marleen McNulty, who has stringy hair which she never washes and who says, "Oh, I get it," ten minutes after everyone else has finished laughing at a joke — even Marleen is going.

Well. *(Folds dish towel into a triangle, ties it around neck to form a sling, and puts one arm in the sling.)* I have decided not to dwell on the reasons why I'm not going. Instead, I will fix it so that I couldn't possibly go, no matter how many people were standing in line to go with me.

There. That looks realistic. No one would expect me to go to the dance like this. When they ask me what happened, I'll say I sprained my wrist and have to keep my arm in this sling for a couple of days. Better yet, I'll say I broke my wrist — no, I broke my *arm* — that really sounds impressive. How did I break it? I'll say I was doing something dangerous — heroic, even. I might as well get all the attention I can.

(Practicing the speech) "I broke it when I dove into the shallow end of our neighbor's swimming pool to save their little boy. He's only eighteen months old and he can't swim and I just happened to

see him toddling around alone and then I heard the splash, so I climbed the fence and dove in, fully clothed — even my shoes — and rescued him. It was kind of tough giving mouth-to-mouth resuscitation when I knew my arm was broken, but I hung in there until the medics arrived."

Maybe I'd better not say that. It's too easy for someone to check and find out our neighbors don't have a swimming pool. Or a little boy. Let's see . . . *(Practicing speech)* "I broke it helping an elderly woman in a wheelchair. She was rolling down a hill, faster and faster, coming toward me. First I thought she was some kind of daredevil old lady and I tried to get out of her way, but then I heard her yell, 'Help! Help! My brakes are gone!' and I realized she was out of control. The only way I could stop her was to throw myself in front of the wheelchair. She ran over my arm, but it was worth it because I got her stopped. There were tears of gratitude in her eyes as she offered me a five-hundred dollar reward but, of course, I wouldn't take it."

When I look back at my life in years to come, I suppose missing the Seventh-Grade Dance won't be particularly memorable. But I think I know what will be memorable. *(Pats the sling.)* The day I broke my arm.

#16

The Best Years

Adults are always telling me that these are the best years of my life. I'm supposed to savor every moment and appreciate each day because supposedly I'll never have it so good again. Well, if these are the best years, I'm certainly not looking forward to the future. How can these be the best years of my life? Most traumatic, maybe. Most embarrassing, yes. But best? No way!

The people who tell me this either have awfully poor memories or else life is vastly different now than it was when they were my age. I wonder if they ever had to endure a junior-high locker room. The first time I had to change into P.E. clothes — and afterwards, take a shower — in front of everyone, I wanted to melt into the floor and disappear.

There are no secrets in a locker room. If you wear a padded bra, at least six people are sure to notice it. If you don't need padding because you're a C-cup naturally, six*teen* people will notice that. And if you don't need any bra at all, you're really in trouble.

In my opinion, it's cruel to require showers after P.E. I'd rather sit all day in my sweaty gym clothes and stink to high heaven than to undress in front of so many people. Some kids actually leave their underwear on in the shower rather than expose themselves to all those staring eyes. This creates other difficulties when they get dressed.

The locker room isn't the only problem in my life. There is also lack of sufficient time for communication with my friends. There's no time to talk after school because we have to get on the school bus or else we miss our ride home. So we call each other as soon as we get home, but we'll just barely talk for any time at all when one or the other of us will be told to get off the phone. My mother is fond of reminding me that I saw Suzy in school all day and so I shouldn't have to tie up the phone talking to her. Nobody in my family understands that even though Suzy and I went to school together, we didn't actually see each other and we certainly didn't have any time to talk.

The most terrible things happen to me. We had our pictures taken for the school annual and mine are awful. I look like a nerd. They are so ugly I wouldn't even show the proofs to Suzy. I wanted to get them retaken, but my parents said the pictures are fine just the way they are and there was no need to go to the time and expense of retakes. Fine the way they are! With my hair sticking out and that stupid look on my face. When I protested that my picture is the ugliest picture I've ever seen in my life, my brother said cameras don't lie. I'm not going to buy an annual this year, and the day the annuals come out, I plan to stay home sick.

Yesterday I got grounded, just because my math teacher sent home a progress report that said I'm not working up to my potential. I *am* working up to my potential; the teacher just doesn't know it because I can't always turn in my assignments. It isn't my fault. Once, my locker partner borrowed my math book and my assignment was in it, and once, I forgot my locker combination and couldn't get the door open to get any of my papers, and once, I did the assignment but forgot to bring it to school with me, and once . . . oh, never mind. Now I'm grounded and I've lost my telephone privileges for a week and I can't go to the football game Friday night and anybody who thinks these are the best years of my life is just plain dumb.

Part Two:

MONOLOGS
FOR
BOYS

#17

Too Young for This;
Too Old for That

I am presently in what the psychologists refer to as The Awkward Age. That means I'm not a little kid any longer, but I'm not grown up yet, either. It also means that my parents can't decide which category I belong in. The result of their indecision is very confusing and if they aren't careful, I'm going to end up needing one of those psychologists.

For example, according to my mother, I am too old for many of the activities I still enjoy. I am too old to go trick-or-treating on Halloween. I am too old to spy on my sister when she comes home from a date. I am too old to swipe apples from Mrs. Munster's tree.

Besides being too old, I am also old enough to know better. *(Mimic a scolding adult:)* " __(Name)__ ! You are old enough to know better than to wear those muddy shoes on the carpet." " __(Name)__ ! You are old enough to know better than to let the parakeet out of his cage when the cat's indoors." *(Helpless shrug)* On the other hand, I am much too young for many of the things I would like to do. According to my parents, I am too young to attend an unchaperoned party. I am too young to go shopping downtown alone. I am too young to attend a movie that's rated PG unless my mother has read a review of it.

The bad part about all this is that there is no reasonable explanation for which things I'm too old for and which I'm too young for. I never know what to expect. Now, I am not an unreasonable person. Nor am I stupid. I know I'm too young to get married and I know I'm too old to pick my nose in public. I do have some common sense. But no one — least of all my parents — gives me credit for that.

My father says, "You are old enough to do your share of the work around here."

My mother says, "You are much too young to run the power lawn mower alone."

He says, "Can't you read anything but comic books? You're old enough to stretch your mind a little."

She says, "Where on earth did you get that magazine? You're too young to read that sort of thing."

Do you know what I think? I think my parents are trying too hard to raise the perfect kid. And the next time they say I'm too young for this or too old for that, I plan to tell them so.

"You think I'm going to turn out perfect?" I'll say. "Ha! You're old enough to know better."

#18

Goodbye, Grandma

My grandma's leaving today. She's going to live in a nursing home. Mom's taking her there. Mom tells me it's for the best, that Grandma will get good care there — but I heard her tell Dad that this is the hardest thing she's ever done in her whole life.

Grandma isn't like she used to be. When I was a little kid, Grandma played games with me. When I played games with my brothers, I always lost, but when I played with Grandma, I always won. We played Old Maid and Go Fish and a special game that she made up just for me, called Kevin's Game. We both promised never, ever to teach it to anyone else and I never did.

We used to bake cookies together, too, and she'd let me really help, not just watch. I got to break the egg into the bowl and chop the nuts and mix the dough. I even got to put the cookie sheets in the oven. Then we'd eat warm cookies and drink milk and talk about neat stuff like how snakes get a drink of water.

It isn't like that anymore. Grandma can't bake cookies because she doesn't remember how. She doesn't remember lots of things, even important things like who I am. How can she forget that? I'm Kevin, her youngest grandchild! But sometimes she calls me Bill and I know she thinks I'm Uncle Bill, my mother's brother.

Mom says Grandma has a brain disease and she can't help behaving like she does and that we must be patient with her and take care of her. I try to be patient, but it isn't always easy. One day she took my new radio out of my room and carried it out to the back yard and left it there, in the rain. My radio was ruined. I know she didn't do it to be mean, but still, it was hard not to be mad at her. When I think how Grandma used to be and how she is now, I feel all sick inside.

Grandma will be safe at the nursing home, Mom says. And the people there are trained to do things like get her dressed and give her a bath. I wouldn't want anyone getting me dressed or giving me a bath.

Grandma has to wear diapers now — just like a baby. I would hate that! I don't know if Grandma hates it or not, because she can't talk much anymore, and when she does talk, it doesn't make any sense; it's kind of a jabber.

She used to tell me neat stories. She made up a character named Mighty Kevin who looked just like me. Mighty Kevin had wonderful adventures. He could make himself invisible — a talent he got from eating fresh vegetables. Mighty Kevin once saved a dog from drowning and he put out a forest fire all by himself. He even went along on one of the space shuttles and helped the astronauts find their way back to earth.

Of course, Mighty Kevin also kept his room clean and helped his mom do the dishes and never goofed off in school. I never minded those parts because the rest of the stories were so exciting and because Mighty Kevin was alway smarter and stronger than his brothers were.

My grandma is leaving today. But my *real* grandma, the one who played games and baked cookies and told me Mighty Kevin stories, is already gone. She left — a little bit at a time — and do you know something? I sure do miss her.

#19

The Efficient Baby-Sitter

When Mrs. Anderson asked me to baby-sit, I was so thrilled didn't even ask how much she intended to pay me. I figured anything as better than nothing, which was how much money I had when he called. Nobody ever asked me to baby-sit before. I have two lder sisters and they sit for people all the time. If Barbara is usy when a customer calls, the customer asks if Janet can do . If Janet has a job when someone calls, the people ask for arbara. Nobody ever asked for me. Is there some law that says irls make better baby-sitters than boys? Week after week, Janet nd Barbara raked in the money on Friday and Saturday nights hile I sat home, penniless and bored.

So you can see why I jumped at the chance when Mrs. Anderson sked if I would like to baby-sit with Frankie, Howard and Brendon. he was going to a luncheon and told me to come to her house at oon. I was determined to do an outstanding job. I would be the 1ost efficient sitter she'd ever had.

I got there right on time, but Mrs. Anderson was waiting r me out in front, as if I was late. She told me the boys were eating 1nch and she'd be home by four. Then she got in her car and started 1e engine. She seemed in a hurry to leave so I waved and went 1side.

Mrs. Anderson was wrong. The boys were not eating their 1nch. They were throwing their lunch at each other. This might ot have been so bad if they had bologna sandwiches, but they had paghettios. Frankie had Spaghettios in his hair, Howard had a ig splotch of Spaghettios on the front of his shirt and Brendon 'as just winding up and taking aim at the kitchen window.

"Cut that out!" I yelled, as loud as I could.

"We don't like Spaghettios," Brendon said.

"Then don't eat them," I told him. "Feed them to the dog or ut them down the garbage disposal, but quit throwing them around 1e kitchen."

Frankie and Howard had a fight over who got to put the Spaghettios down the disposal first. Brendon had a temper tantru because he wanted to give his to the dog, but they didn't have a d and their cat wouldn't come when we called her.

I finally got everyone calmed down and *I* ate Brendon Spaghettios. I used paper towels and Windex to get the toma sauce out of Frankie's hair and I decided Howard could just we a dirty shirt the rest of the afternoon.

I told the boys I'd play a game with them and after mu wrangling, they agreed to play hide-and-seek. They wanted play inside, but I told them we had to play in the back yard. Th way, the house would stay clean and Mrs. Anderson would ask m to baby-sit again. Maybe she'd even pay me extra.

Frankie said he would be "it" first, which surprised me. thought they'd want me to be "it." Frankie closed his eyes and start counting to twenty. I hid behind a big stack of old newspapers the garage. I heard Frankie yell, "Ready or not, here I come!" a then I didn't hear anything more. I waited and waited, but never came near the garage. Finally, I stood up and peeked out t garage door. The boys were nowhere in sight.

I began to feel a little nervous so I stepped outside in fu view. Nobody said, "I spy." Nobody said anything at all. The ya was silent, but a terrible banging was coming from upstairs on t front side of the Anderson's house. I ran to the back door; it w locked. I raced around to the front door. It was locked, too. I pound on the door with both fists and shouted, "Hey, you guys. Ope the door and let me in."

"Go away," they yelled. "We don't want a baby-sitter."

I tried to pick the locks. I looked under the doormat for spare key. I tried to jimmy open the bathroom window. I begg and pleaded with the boys to let me in.

When Mrs. Anderson got home at 5:30, I was sitting o the front steps, rehearsing the speech I planned to give her. wasn't necessary. When I told her they'd locked me out, she ju hrugged, handed me my pay, and said she'd call me again. Then he got out her key and opened the front door. I have no idea what he found inside.

Whatever it was, it must not have been too terrible because he called the next day and asked me to baby-sit again. I told her I was busy. No amount of money in the world is worth another afternoon with Frankie, Howard and Brendon.

#20

Little Red, the Hood

Just because I'm a wolf, everyone assumes I'm the bad gu. People say, "Poor Little Red Riding Hood. Poor old Grannie."

Ha! If the truth were known, Little Red and Grannie woul be arrested for fraud, perjury and intent to deceive a police office Those two women are real con artists, but Little Red's cute and ca scream hysterically, so everyone believed her version of wha happened. Nobody would listen to me. Well, I think it's time th real story got told. I'm tired of taking the rap.

It began late one Sunday afternoon, deep in the woods. Nov I live in the woods, you understand. These are *my* woods — wel mine and the bank's. I have another fourteen years to go on m mortgage. The point is, the woods are my home and Little Red wa trespassing. Naturally, when I saw her running across my propert; I stopped her and asked what she was doing.

You probably think she told me she was on her way to vis her sick grandmother. Wrong. She told me the most incredib thing had just happened. She said she was walking through th woods, looking for wild flowers, when she spotted something hidde under a bush. Being curious, she looked closer and was astonishe to find several stacks of thousand-dollar bills. Since there was n one around to claim the money, she put it in her basket and wa on her way to her sick grannie's house to call the police. She lifte one corner of the napkin which covered her basket and gave m a quick peek. There were bundles and bundles of cash, neatl bound with rubber bands. I'd never seen so much money. A littl prickle of excitement ran down my back, clear to the tip of my tail

"Are you sure you want to call the police?" I asked he "They'll just confiscate the money and probably never find th owner. Think what you could do with all that cash."

She looked at me and blinked her big blue eyes innocently. Oh, I can't keep it," she said. "I'd be too nervous to spend thousand-ollar bills. I usually only have tens and twenties."

I couldn't believe she was serious. I never had a thousand-ollar bill, either, but I sure wasn't too nervous to spend one.

Then she said it's too bad it was Sunday and the banks ere closed, because otherwise she'd be willing to trade me all he money in her basket for whatever I had in smaller bills.

Now, that statement made my fur stand on end. I didn't now how much cash she had under that napkin, but I'd glimpsed lot of little bundles. I told her it didn't matter if it was Sunday. I ad a bank card for the cash machine. I offered to draw out everything 1 my account and we'd trade. She asked me how much I had nd I told her about two thousand. Then she gave me that innocent mile and said she wouldn't be at all afraid to spend two thousand 1 tens and twenties.

By then, my heart was pounding. I had visions of myself riving around the woods in my new Rolls Royce. Maybe spending he winter in Hawaii or Florida.

Little Red and I hurried to the First Interforest Bank and got out my little plastic card and punched the numbers. As the ens and twenties came out of the machine, I handed them to Red nd she tucked them in the pocket of her cape. It took awhile, but ventually my account was empty and Red's pocket was bulging. he handed me the basket and suggested I wait until I get home o open it, in case anyone dishonest was watching. Then we shook ands and went our separate ways. I took the shortcut back to the oods, locked my lair, and opened the basket. It was quite a shock. here were lots of bundles, but they weren't thousand-dollar bills. hey were pieces of paper, cut in the size of bills. The only stack hat had a real bill on top was the one in the corner where I'd ad my quick peek, and that bill was one hundred dollars, not one housand. I was furious. I'd been bilked out of my life savings!

I rushed to Grannie's house and it wasn't locked, so I went inside. The bed was empty; Grannie apparently had a miraculous recovery. I quickly put on Grannie's nightgown and nightcap and climbed in the bed to wait for Little Red.

You know the rest of the story. Red showed up with an undercover agent disguised as a woodchopper. Grannie jumped out of the closet and the two of them concocted that terrible story about me. Before I could protest, I was handcuffed and on my way to the slammer.

And do you know the worst part of all? The part that never made it to the storybooks? First Interforest Bank hit me with thirty two dollars in service charges for overdrawing my account.

#21

Day of Liberation

This is the happiest day of my life.

No prisoner ever yearned for freedom more than I yearned
r mine. No iron bars have ever been more confining than the ones I
st escaped. I've been behind them for two years. Two years! For
o long, excruciating years, I haven't even been allowed to chew
stick of gum.

Today I am reborn. I am a brand-new person. I am not the
y I was yesterday or last week or last month. I am changed. I am free!

Do you know what it's like to kiss a girl when there are
rips of metal between your lips and hers? It isn't easy, or pleasant.
ave yet to meet the girl who gets turned on by strands of wire.
t tonight — ah tonight is going to be different. Pucker up,
veetheart, here I come.

And food. Oh, when I think of the food I've missed in the
st two years. My family has a garden, and late in the summer my
other always cooks corn-on-the-cob. She puts the water on to boil
fore she goes out to pick the corn. Then she husks the corn and
ops it right in the pot. Twenty minutes after they're plucked
m the stalk, those sweet, juicy ears of corn are being consumed,
ushed with butter and a dash of salt.

Only they weren't consumed by me. Not last year, or the
ar before.

Today is different. Today I can eat anything I want. Make
four ears of corn for me, or maybe five. I may eat corn-on-the-cob
r breakfast tomorrow.

If I live to be ninety years old, I'll look back at my life and
obably I'll remember my wedding day and the births of my children
d maybe I'll remember some special accomplishments or events.
t for sure I'll remember today because today is unlike any other
y I will ever experience.

I could sing and shout. I could dance in the streets. I lo
everyone in the entire world, even my little brother. I can laug
again, not just smile politely.

So bring on the sweet corn and the pretty girls who wa
to be kissed by an expert. Here I am, world, without the meta

Pass the gum, friends. Today, I got my braces off.

#22

New Year's Resolution

Every year my mother makes a list of New Year's resolutions. Every year, the list is the same. She vows to lose ten pounds, to exercise regularly, and to keep the refrigerator clean so we don't find moldy leftovers.

I don't know why she bothers to write out a new list each year. It would be easier to make a photocopy of last year's list. When I suggested this, she hinted strongly that *I* could benefit from making a few resolutions of my own.

I knew she was right so I told her my New Year's resolution was to clean my room and keep it clean. She said she was glad to hear it.

I began with my desk. I hadn't been able to get the two top drawers shut for several months, so they seemed a good place to start. I removed both of them from the desk and dumped the contents on my bed. It made quite a heap. There were all the shells I gathered on the beach last summer, the marbles that Hughie Lange traded me for my old felt-tip markers, the baseball cards that are duplicates of the ones I already have but which I need to save in case I ever have a chance to trade them for some I don't have, and the plans for the fort which Hughie and I are going to build someday on the vacant lot next to his house. There were also some comic books, two incomplete decks of cards, last year's birthday cards, two school reports that I got A's on, and twenty or thirty broken crayons, all loose. There was an old bag of M & M's with a few candies left in the bottom. I figured they were my reward for being so tidy and I ate them while I read all the old comic books.

I decided the best place to keep the duplicate baseball cards would be on my closet shelf, since that's where the rest of my baseball card collection is. In order to make room on the shelf, I had to remove a few other items. I took down the shoeshine kit that I made the summer I decided to open my own business, and the kite that needs a new tail, and the box of rocks that I found when I visited my cousin who has a rock collection. We went on long hikes, looking for agates and fossils, but I found lots of other pretty rocks, too, and someday I'm going to look all of them up in a rock book and find out what they are.

I needed something to put the duplicate baseball cards in but I couldn't find an empty box anywhere, so I dumped the shoeshine kit out onto the floor. There was black shoe polish, brown shoe polish, some old rags, two brushes and the sign I'd made which said "SHOESHINE. 50¢."

When I started filing the duplicate baseball cards in the shoeshine box, I quickly realized I had two kinds of cards: new ones in good condition, and old ratty ones. It only made sense to keep them separate, so in order to get a second box, I emptied all the rocks onto the floor next to the shoe polish. Then I started putting the old, ratty baseball cards in the box marked "Rocks" and the new, good baseball cards in the box marked "Shoeshine Kit."

Almost immediately, I discovered that I had three old ratty Johnny Bench cards from the same year so I opened the bottom desk drawer to get a rubber band so I could keep all three cards together. The rubber bands were not right on top where I thought they were. I dug around in the drawer for awhile and finally took it out and emptied the contents on my bed, along with the broken crayons, the fort plans, the shells and all the rest.

The rubber bands were not in that drawer, after all, but the remains of my old Tinker Toy set were. I hadn't seen those Tinker Toys since I was in kindergarten.

I sat on the floor — there wasn't room to sit on the bed — and started putting them together. I thought maybe Hughie and I could make a model of our future fort out of my old Tinker Toys.

That's what I was doing when my mother came to tell me dinner was ready. She looked at my bed and at the floor. She picked up one of the shoeshine rags, sniffed it, and put it down again. Then e asked what had happened to my resolution to clean my room.

"That's what I'm doing," I told her.

I could see she didn't believe me, but what can you expect om someone who has to make the same resolution over and over, ery single year?

#23

Riding the Merry-Go-Round

When we go to the County Fair tomorrow, David and Joh are going to ride on the Black Hole. They want me to ride on i too, to prove I'm not scared. I don't really want to go on the Blac Hole. To tell the truth, I don't see much point in whirling upsid down in the dark until you're so dizzy you get sick to your stomacl But all the guys want to ride on the Black Hole, just so they ca say they did it.

Personally, I'd rather ride the merry-go-round. I've alway loved the merry-go-round, especially the music. It's calliope musi with an oom-pah-pah beat, and when it drifts out across the fairground it's a happy sound, not like the screaming that comes from th Black Hole. Merry-go-round music always makes me smile.

Riding the merry-go-round is a pleasure unlike any othe. First there is the big decision of which animal to ride on. Sha I choose the white horse, with the red plume on his head? Or th big black one, with the painted gold blanket? I'm always tempte by the cat with the fish in his mouth, and once I rode a carous that had a seahorse and a white rabbit. I rode it twice, so I coul have a turn to sit on each of them.

Usually, I want to ride a horse, but I must decide whethe I want an inside horse, an outside horse, or one in the middl There are advantages to each. If you sit on an inside horse, yo can see your reflection in the mirrors around the calliope. If yo have an outside horse, it's easier to wave to your parents or you friends each time you complete a full circle. And when you hav a middle horse, you feel like you're really in the center of a whol pack of horses, riding along together.

Most often I pick an outside horse because I like to watc the fairgrounds whirling past me as I go round and round.

If I can, I choose one that's in the "up" position becaus it's harder to get on. You have to put one foot in the stirrup and gras

1e pole hard and swing the other leg up over the horse's back. It's
asier to do when the horse is in the "down" position, but not as
itisfying.

Once mounted, I grasp the pole and wait for the music to
egin. The best moment of all is when the music first starts and the
1erry-go-round begins to turn and my horse starts to move. Then
 goes faster and faster and pretty soon someone comes to take
1e ticket which I have squeezed between the palm of my hand
1d the pole.

Up and down and around and around, with the wind in my
1ce. Sometimes I close my eyes and listen to the music and feel
1yself moving. Sometimes I pet my horse or scratch him behind
1e ears. Sometimes I stand up, with my feet in the stirrups and
1y knees pressed tight against the horse's belly.

When I finish a ride on the merry-go-round, I never feel
ck to my stomach. I feel exhilarated. And I always want to go
1ck and ride again.

Last year, I went on all the scary rides with David and
1hn, just to prove I wasn't chicken, and when I went home, I felt
1eated. I'd been to the fair and spent my money and missed the
1erry-go-round, the best ride of all.

This year, I'm not going to do it. I've decided if I really want
 show some courage, I'll admit I prefer the merry-go-round to
1e Black Hole. David and John can get sick if they want to, but
m going to find the calliope music and take a ride on a big,
hite horse. An outside one.

#24

Little League Dreamer

Someday, I'm going to coach a Little League baseball team. When I do, I'm going to let everybody have a turn to play in every game. No. Not just a turn to play; everybody's going to have a turn to *start*.

I go to all the practices, but I hardly ever get to play in the games. I just sit on the bench and watch and yell for the other guys. Oh, once in a while I get to go in, but it's usually the last inning and we're either so far ahead that there's no way we can blow it or else we're so far behind that there's no way we can catch up. If the game is close at all, I never get a turn to play.

On the first day of practice, the coach asked all of us what position we wanted to play. Most of the guys wanted to be the pitcher, but I said I wanted first base, so he put me at first base. I was doing great until two ground balls got by me. Then I caught a pop fly, but when I threw to third, to get the runner there, I overthrew and the runner scored. After that, I didn't get to play first base anymore, which really isn't fair because those were just mistakes and I would never make them again.

Although I prefer to play first base, I'd be happy with center field or any other position. I'm not fussy.

The coach says he puts Ricky Anders at first base because Ricky's arm is better than mine and so is his batting average. That may be true, but the reason Ricky's arm is better and he gets more hits is because he plays more. I'd be a better hitter if I got a chance more often. I admit I don't hit so well in practice, but that's different. I know I'd be great if I had a chance to hit during a game.

Once, I actually got up to bat during the last inning of a game. The batter ahead of me walked, so there was a runner on base. I knew it was my big chance. I couldn't win the game — we were already eleven runs ahead — but if I could hit a home run, it would show the coach how good I really am. Maybe he'd even let me start next time.

I didn't get the home run. I didn't even get a single. What I got was a strike-out, on a called strike three when I wasn't even swinging. I'll never make that mistake again, either, but the coach just won't listen.

It's such a waste of talent. I know I could be an All-Star baseball player, if only I got to play more often.

#25

The Shoe Box

When I was not quite seven years old, I made my father shoe box for his Christmas gift. It was no ordinary shoe box; thi was a wooden box, built from scraps of three-quarter-inch plywoo that I found in my father's workshop. I glued them together i a rectangular shape that was about four feet long and two feet wid I thought he could put the shoe box in his closet and keep h shoes in it.

After I got all the pieces glued together, the box looked rathe plain. I wanted to paint it, but I couldn't get the can of paint ope by myself, and since the shoe box was going to be a surprise, didn't want to ask for help. I used colored felt-tip markers to dra designs on the sides of the box — a Christmas tree and a San Claus and some stars. In big letters on one side, I wrote, in m very best printing, "If you don't know what this is, ask Bobby On the other side, I wrote, "Do you know that I love you, Daddy?"

I hid the shoe box in the furnace room so no one would se it. I didn't have to worry too much about anyone finding it becaus I didn't make the box until the day before Christmas and everybod was busy and not paying much attention to me or to the furna room.

The next morning, my whole family gathered around th Christmas tree. Mom, Dad, my two older brothers, Justin ar Mark, and my Grandma Helen. I still didn't bring the shoe b upstairs because it was too big to wrap. My plan was to wa until we'd opened all our gifts and then I would go get the sh box and bring it in and give it to my father. I got more excited thinkir about that than I did when I saw my own packages. It was th first time I'd ever had a gift to give that was mine alone. Nobo helped me select it, nobody gave me money to pay for it, nobo took me shopping. Nobody but me even knew it was there.

But as the morning proceeded, I began to have doubts. Grandma Helen gave my father a new camera and he was so excited that he quit opening his presents and started taking pictures of all of us, until Mom made him stop and open his own gifts. Justin and Mark are both a lot older than I and have part-time jobs, so their presents were special, too. Justin gave Dad the new screwdrivers he'd been wanting and Mark gave him a whole box of golf balls. Mom gave him a cordless electric drill.

As I sat there looking at all those wonderful presents and seeing how much my father liked them, I wondered if I should even bring the shoe box upstairs. Who would want a silly old box, glued together out of leftover lumber, when he had a camera and new tools and golf balls? Maybe I should just leave it in the furnace room. I could go down after Christmas and take it apart and nobody would know anything about it.

But if I did that, I wouldn't have any present for my father. He would think I didn't get him anything at Christmas. I decided it would be better to give him the dumb old shoe box than to have him think I didn't get him any present at all.

I went down to the furnace room and got the shoe box and dragged it upstairs. It wasn't easy to do; the box was both big and heavy. I carried it into the living room and put it down in front of my father. Then I braced myself, in case Justin and Mark laughed.

They didn't, though. Everyone was quiet while my father looked at the shoe box. Then he stood up and walked all the way around it and read the writing on both sides out loud.

"It's a shoe box," I said, in case he couldn't tell. "To keep all your shoes in."

"It's a *beautiful* shoe box," my father said, and he sat down on the floor beside me and gave me a bear hug.

"I made it myself," I told him.

Later that afternoon, he took the shoe box into his bedroom and I helped him put all his shoes in it. There was plenty of room. He told me the shoe box was the best Christmas present of all and that he planned to keep his shoes in it forever and ever.

#26

Manure Measles

I'm a city boy, through and through. Born and raised in the concrete jungle. I've always liked the city, but my mama has a hankering to live in the country. Not a farm, necessarily; just a few acres of land with clean, fresh air and her own vegetable garden.

When I was five, we were invited to visit Mama's great-aunt Minnie, who lives in a small rural town in Wisconsin. Aunt Minnie paid our train fare, and Mama and I spent two weeks breathing clean, fresh air. Mama loved it. I was bored silly.

I was bored, that is, until the day I met Ham Bone. Ham Bone was two years older than I and he lived in the farmhouse at the edge of Aunt Minnie's town. We met quite by accident when we both reached for the last Fudgsicle in the freezer case of Davidson's Grocery. Ham Bone beat me to it. Then he asked me my name and where I lived and I asked his name and where he lived and when he said he lived on a farm, I asked if I could go home with him and see the cows. He seemed surprised by that request, but he said it was OK with him.

When we got there, the cows were out to pasture, which was disappointing, but at the far end of the barn, just on the other side of a low fence, there was the biggest, deepest, most wonderful-looking puddle I'd ever seen. It was brown and thick and it glistened in the sunshine.

"That's some puddle," I said to Ham Bone.

He looked at me like I was a retardo. "That's manure," he said. "Pig manure."

Manure. I repeated the word slowly, rolling it on my tongue. It was an excellent word, a fitting name for such a fine puddle. I wondered what kind of splash it would make if I threw a rock in the pig manure puddle.

"Try it and find out," Ham Bone said.

I found a small rock on the ground, carried it to the edge of the puddle, climbed the fence, leaned over and dropped the rock. Plop! It sank out of sight, with a satisfying plunk.

I looked around for a bigger rock and found one the size of a baseball. Once again I climbed the fence and dropped the rock. This one not only made a fine, schlurpey sound as it sank, it also made the manure splash into the air, splattering brown dots on my shoes.

By then, I was addicted. I searched for bigger and bigger rocks, while Ham Bone egged me on. Finally I found one that measured almost a foot in diameter. I could barely lift it. Somehow I managed to hoist it onto one hip and, dragging my foot behind me, I made my way to the puddle, struggled up the fence, leaned over and let the rock slide in. It made a deep, resonant *ker-plunk*. Droplets of manure came flying upward, onto my face, my hands, my hair. Big brown circles dotted my clothing and dripped from my arms.

I grinned at Ham Bone. "I have the manure measles," I told him.

Ham Bone doubled over with laughter, like it was the funniest thing he'd ever heard in his life. All the way back to Aunt Minnie's house, I kept chanting, "I've got the man-u-er mea-sles. I've got the man-u-er mea-sles."

Aunt Minnie took one look at me and screamed.

Mama made me take two baths while she washed all my clothes. She kept saying she'd brought me to the country to breathe clean, pure air and why was I bent on contaminating myself?

We came home the next day and I was glad to be back in the city. Still, I sometimes sit at the window and pretend that instead of a traffic light on the corner, there is a big, thick, brown puddle of pig manure, just waiting to have a rock dropped in it.

#27

Love Letter to Suzy

Suzy Littlejohn is new at our school this year and I fell in love with her the very first day. She has blond curly hair and big brown eyes, but the real reason I fell for her so fast was her pimples. Not that I find pimples particularly attractive. I get them myself and I hate them. That first day, Suzy's face was really broken out — probably from being nervous about starting a new school — and when she walked in the door, some smart-mouth in the front row said loudly, "Look who's here. It's Pimple Puss in person."

Most girls would have been all embarrassed and maybe even started to cry. Not Suzy. She just gave the guy a sparkling smile and said, "Do you always try to make newcomers feel so welcome?"

It took a lot of guts for her to say that, and I decided right then that Suzy was someone special. This feeling was reinforced a week later when my dog, Goliath, followed me to school and jumped up on Suzy and left muddy paw prints all over her coat. He also left a pile of dog-doo in the school yard and, unfortunately, Suzy stepped in it when she was trying to back away from him.

I couldn't offer to clean her shoe because I had to take Goliath home before someone called the dog pound. When I apologized, Suzy said she likes dogs and Goliath was just being friendly.

I had a chocolate-almond bar at home, so when I put Goliath in, I got my candy bar and took it to Suzy, for a surprise. I slipped it into her notebook while she was sharpening her pencil. How was I supposed to know she would open her notebook right in front of Miss Marston, who is the crabbiest teacher in the whole school and who has a strict rule about No Food In Class? Suzy had to stay after for a week.

When the All School Dance was announced, I knew I wanted to go with Suzy. I was afraid to ask her, though. I was afraid to ask anyone. I've never gone to a dance before. I never asked a girl to go anywhere with me and it takes a lot of courage. What if she says *no?*

I was trying to get up my nerve when I read a magazine article titled, "How to Write the Perfect Love Letter." According to the article, a woman who receives a love letter is so thrilled, she'll say *yes* to anything.

I decided to write a love letter to Suzy — the perfect love letter — and at the end of the letter, I'd ask her to go to the dance with me. The love letter would guarantee she'd say *yes,* and at the same time spare me the agony of asking her in person.

The article said to begin the love letter by stating the first thing I noticed when I saw her. That was easy. I scribbled in my notebook, feeling encouraged. Next I was supposed to complete the sentence, "When I think about you, I remember . . . " That was easy, too.

The third part was harder. The letter was supposed to give a reason why I like to be with her. The article suggested that I mention a past experience which was particularly vivid in my memory and say I hoped to do it again. "Stir her memory," the article said. "Make her feel nostalgic about your shared past." I didn't know what *nostalgic* meant, and Suzy and I hadn't shared many experiences in the past, but I did the best I could. Then I copied the love letter onto clean notebook paper.

It went like this:

Dear Suzy: The first thing I noticed about you was your pimples. When I think about you, I remember how Miss Marston caught you with my chocolate bar. I like to be with you because we've shared the experience of Goliath's dog-doo and I hope we'll do it again. Will you go to the All School Dance with me?

The article didn't say how to sign my name, but since this was a love letter, I signed it, *With love.*

I don't know what went wrong. Suzy wasn't thrilled at all. She tore the letter into little pieces and hasn't spoken to me since.

Maybe I should have signed it, *Sincerely yours.*

#28

I'm Not My Brother; I'm Me

My brother, Steve, is four years older than I am. He's always been a four-point student and played center on the basketball team. One game, he scored thirty-two points and set a new school record.

My brother, Mark, is three years older than I am. He tends to be on the rowdy side and got into trouble for stealing another school's mascot and trying to overthrow the student council.

It isn't easy to follow two guys like that. People expect me to be like my brothers, whether I am or not. On my first day in Mr. Swenson's chemistry class, he took me aside after class and informed me that he would absolutely not tolerate any experiments with the Bunsen burners other than those which were class assignments. He made it quite clear that if he caught me so much as looking at a Bunsen burner, I could expect immediate detention and would spend it scraping gum off the bottoms of the tables in the library.

I could only blink and nod at him. At that point, I didn't even know what a Bunsen burner was and I certainly didn't know that Mark had once set off a series of minor explosions which resulted in the fire department sending two trucks to school and Mr. Swenson being reprimanded by the principal. For the next two weeks, even though I liked chemistry, I was scared to look at anything in the room for fear I'd end up under a library table with a scraper in my hand.

I had a different problem in geometry. No matter how hard I tried, all those angles and formulas didn't make sense to me. I did my homework, but it was usually wrong, and when Miss Scutter explained it in class, I still didn't understand. So one day I stayed after school to get some extra help and instead I got a lecture.

"It's obvious," Miss Scutter told me, "that you are not working up to your potential. There's no excuse for the number of errors on your last test. You simply aren't trying."

Her angry attitude surprised me because my friend, Allen, had just as many mistakes, and when he asked for extra help, Miss Scutter was delighted and spent a whole hour showing him how to do the problems.

Then Miss Scutter continued her tirade and I understood. "Your brother, Steve, always got straight A's in my class," she said, "and I expect you to do the same."

I transferred out of geometry the next day and took Current Events instead. I picked Current Events because it's taught by a new faculty member, someone who never met either of my brothers.

Why can't people wait until they know me before deciding what I'm like? They don't, though. The basketball coach was overjoyed when I turned out. He assumed I would be fast and well-coordinated and deadly at the free throw line. When I didn't make the team, I think he was more disappointed than I was.

The chaperones at the school dance spent half the night watching me because they expected me to pull some prank, like Mark always did. I felt like I was on parole without ever committing a crime.

Steve and Mark are both in college now. Steve got a scholarship to Stanford and Mark attends one of the state universities. Mark got all A's and B's his first semester. Not only that, he was elected vice president of the freshman class.

I got to wondering what happened to change him so much. I couldn't figure it out, so when he came home during midwinter break, I asked him how come he wasn't getting into trouble anymore. He told me he used to cause problems in high school because he got sick of everyone expecting him to be exactly like Steve! He said he wasted so much time proving who he wasn't, he never found out who he was.

I'm not going to make Mark's mistake. From now on, I'm going to be me and if anyone mentions my brothers, I'll remind them that I'm not Steve and I'm not Mark. I'm Jonathon.

#29

Reunited Twins

I hope his plane isn't late. I don't think I can stand to wait one extra minute. Do you think we'll recognize each other? But that's a silly question; it's like asking if I'd recognize myself. Of course we'll recognize each other. We're twins, aren't we? How could we not recognize each other? Still, I haven't seen him since we were born.

It's odd, when you think about it. All those years when I wished I had a brother and I never knew he existed. He didn't know about me, either. We wouldn't have found out now except his parents — that is, the people who adopted him — were killed in a car accident, and when Bill went through all their papers, he found the adoption records.

He knew he was adopted — I've always known, too — but he didn't know he was a twin. Neither did I, until last week when Bill called and asked if he could come for a visit.

I think my folks were secretly afraid that if Bill and I knew about each other we might decide to try to find our birth mother, but I don't want to do that. I love my parents and I see no reason to hunt for anyone else.

I do want to see Bill. After being an only child all these years, it's exciting to know I have a brother. A twin brother, no less. I wonder if he'll be tall or short. I wonder if his hair is brown like mine or if he's blond.

Here comes his plane. He's landed!

What if we don't like each other? What if he's stupid or mean or into drugs? It could happen. He sounded OK on the telephone, but that doesn't mean anything. Maybe he'll have body odor and radical ideas and tell dirty jokes in front of my parents. Maybe I shouldn't have said I wanted to meet him. I'll have to introduce him to all my friends and later they'll say, *"That* was your twin brother? What a nerd!" And . . .

Oh! The passengers are getting off. There he is! He looks exactly like me, even his haircut. *(Waves tentatively.)* Bill?

He sees me. Here he comes. He looks just as nervous as I am.

Hi, Bill. How're you doing, brother?

#30

The Girl that I Marry

I don't plan to get married for a long, long time. But when I do, I'm not jumping into it blindly, just because I happen to fall in love. No, sir. I've seen too many divorces and I'm not about to make a mistake.

I've decided that the secret to a happy marriage is planning. You need to plan well in advance what kind of person you want to marry and then seek her out. If you know what you're looking for and don't date anybody who doesn't qualify, you can't go wrong.

I've started a list of criteria for the person I eventually marry. So far, there are four items on my list.

First of all, my future wife must understand football. It would drive me nuts to live with someone who didn't know the difference between a tight end and quarterback. You can keep your bouncy cheerleader types who jump and yell and agree with whatever you say. Give me a girl who will argue with me when I pick the Rams to win the Super Bowl.

Second, she has to love dogs. Not tolerate, love. Some of my best friends are dogs. They're loyal, fun to be with, and they can keep a secret. If they also shed on the furniture, well, that's a small price to pay for their company. A girl who isn't willing to hold a golden retriever on her lap isn't the right girl for me.

Third, she should adore Twinkies. And chocolate. Ideally, she'll get occasional cravings for something like a hot fudge sundae, cravings so strong that she'll get dressed in the middle of the night and drive through a snow storm until she finds a Baskin-Robbins that's open. I figure if she likes junk food and will go to extreme lengths sometimes to get it, she'll never nag at me to improve my eating habits, and if I decide to leave our cozy hearth in the middle of a TV movie to go after a bag of M &M's, she'll even ride along.

Number four — but it's so important I'm thinking of changing it to number one — my future wife must not mind unmade beds, unwashed dishes and undusted furniture. She will believe me when I tell her it's a verifiable statistic that more apple pies bubble over in clean ovens than in dirty ones because she wants to believe it.

That's her, the girl of my dreams: someone who can't be bothered with housework because she and her dog are busy watching a football game and eating a bag of Hershey's kisses.

I don't know where or when I'll meet this perfect creature but I'm not getting married until I do.

#31

She Hit Me First

I have never figured out why it is that parents don't want their children to fight. Oh, sure, I understand why they don't want the kids to actually hurt each other physically, like break your brother's legs or yank out all your sister's hair. But what's wrong with a good, loud argument? Most kids *like* to fight with their brothers and sisters and they would do it even more than they do already if it didn't bother the parents so much.

I have several fine fights going with my brother and sister. For example, it drives my sister Sharon crazy if she thinks I'm spying on her or eavesdropping on her conversations. The truth is, Sharon doesn't do anything interesting enough to warrant spying or eavesdropping, but it's fun to make her think that's what I'm doing. Whenever I'm bored and have nothing better to do, I'll sit in the hallway outside Sharon's room. That's all I have to do, just sit there, and pretty soon she's yelling at me to quit spying on her. Naturally, I protest that I'm not spying, I am merely sitting in the hall.

Then she'll yell, "Mo-ther! Make him quit spying on me," and I'll call her a tattletale, and then we really get going. Our parents always ignore us at first. I think they hope we'll stop of our own accord, but we never do.

Usually Sharon gets so angry that she starts to cry, which is my cue to call her a crybaby, which is her cue to sock me, which is my cue to sock her back. That's usually when our parents interfere.

You will notice that I do not sock Sharon until after she socks me. There's a good reason for this self-control. When one of my parents comes to find out what the fight is about, I want to be able to say, "She hit me first." That makes it sound like Sharon started the fight, which she did. I was just innocently sitting in the hall, minding my own business.

It isn't quite so easy to fight with my brother Frank. For one thing, Frank is older than I and so he's a more experienced fighter. It's pretty hard to trick Frank into hitting me first, no matter how hard I try.

I've found the best way to start a fight with Frank is to make remarks about his looks. Not *bad* remarks. That would get me in trouble with Mom real fast because she's always saying "If you can't say anything nice, don't say anything at all." So I have to be careful.

I got good results one time by telling Frank that his pimples looked a lot better than they used to. Another time I told him he should wear his green shirt more often because his potbelly didn't show so much.

Best of all is when I hint that Frank and some girl like each other. It doesn't matter which girl I pick. If it's one that Frank doesn't like at all, he gets mad at me for making it up, and if it's a girl Frank really does like, he gets mad at me for blabbing his personal business. Either way, we have a dandy argument and are free to insult each other until someone makes us stop.

He'll call me a creep and I'll call him a squashed worm and he'll say I smell like a cow barn and I'll say he has the IQ of a tomato and he'll say if I was any uglier he could make his fortune selling tickets and I'll say it's too bad he can't afford plastic surgery on his ears, and just about then our parents will holler at us to cut it out.

Like I said, parents just don't want their kids to entertain themselves by fighting. It's too bad, since fighting's so much fun.

Part Three:

MONOLOGS FOR BOYS OR GIRLS

#32

Help! Send Candy Bars!

There is a lot of material being published that tells kids like me how to cope with the terrible things that might happen to us. If I'm walking to school and a stranger drives up and offers me a ride and says he'll give me money, I know what I'm supposed to do. I'm supposed to scream and run away.

I'm glad I know this. I hope I don't ever have to scream and run, but I'm glad I know what to do if something bad like that should happen to me.

However, there's one problem that none of the books ever talks about. We never have special programs about it in school and there aren't any public service announcements on TV. It's a serious problem, though, and widespread. I'm not the only one who's trying to cope without any help; plenty of my friends are suffering, too.

The problem is this: how does a kid like me protect himself *(Herself)* when his *(Her)* mother decides to go on a diet? It's terrible! It's a real shock when this happens, and nobody ever prepared me for it. One day I was able to open our refrigerator and find cold fried chicken and chocolate pudding, and the next day there was nothing but raw cauliflower and yogurt. Yuck! A growing boy *(Girl)* could starve to death eating raw cauliflower and yogurt.

I told my mom I don't want her to diet. I said I love her just the way she is and she said I'm very sweet. "Besides," I said, "most of my friends' moms are fat, too."

I don't think I should have added that last part. She quit telling me how sweet I am and started doing sit-ups.

Our cookie jar is empty. There aren't even any crumbs in the bottom that will stick to my finger if I lick it and rub it around on the inside. I asked what good is a cookie jar if there are never any cookies in it, and I got some song-and-dance about reducing tooth decay. Heck, my teeth are in good shape; it's my stomach that needs help.

For dinner last night we had baked fish, green beans and sliced tomato. I could have as much as I wanted, but who want seconds of baked fish?

We used to have a Goodie Drawer. It was just what th name implies, a drawer in the kitchen where we kept goodies. Ther were usually peanuts and often pretzels and sometimes even bag of candy bars. I love candy bars. I adore candy bars. At leas I used to. Candy bars have been banned from our house ever sinc Mom put on her navy suit and couldn't get the pants zipped.

I suggested that we buy a padlock and put it on the Good: Drawer, and everyone but Mom would know the combination. " you will buy the candy bars," I said, "I will lock them up for you She wouldn't do it. She says she doesn't want to ruin the kitche drawer by putting a lock on it, but I think she doesn't want anyor else eating candy bars if she can't have any.

It is painful to have my mother on a diet. My whole life ha changed. Why don't the school counselors or the child welfar people do something to help? I'll bet thousands of kids are sufferin; just like I am, from candy bar withdrawal. As far as I'm concerne you can forget all the instructions about what to do if somebod tries to abduct me. Instead, tell me what to do when there's nothin in the house to eat.

#33

Applying for a Job

(Carry a piece of paper and a pencil for this scene.) Well, here am, applying for my very first job. Me and about forty-five other eople. Look at that man over there in the suit and tie. He looks ke he's thirty years old. Why would an old man like that apply r a job as a dishwasher in a fast-food restaurant? I'll never get ired if I have to compete with him.

Maybe they'll tell him he's over-qualified for the job. They are won't tell me that. I only hope they don't say I'm under-qualified. hope they even talk to me. That's all I ask, just talk to me. Give e a chance! On the other hand, if they talk to me, they might sk me a bunch of questions I can't answer and then I'll look like n idiot, and nobody's going to hire an idiot to wash their dishes. ot when they have their choice of forty-five people whose brains em to be in good working order.

I guess I'd better quit staring at the other people and fill ut this application form.

Name. I wonder if they want my real name or what everybody alls me. Probably my real name. This is a business form and they robably want my full legal name. Yuck. If I put down Frances *rancis)*, then that's what they'll call me and I won't know they're alking to me. On the other hand, I don't really want my paychecks be made out to Peanut. I know! I'll use my initials. *(Quickly rite down initials.)*

Social Security number. Oh, no! They want a Social Security umber. I don't *have* a Social Security number. I should have applied r one, before I came here. What a dunce I am. I wonder how long takes to get one. I think I'll just make up a number and write it n this application. Who would know the difference? They can't ossibly check out every Social Security number to see if you're ring or not.

But what if I make up a number and then I get the job. They'll withhold money from my paycheck and put it in the wrong Social Security account, and when I'm sixty-five years old I'll be poor and hungry. I'll have to eat dog food and sleep on park benches. Either that, or I'll have to admit I lied. Wouldn't that look great. The first thing I do when I get my new job is go and tell the boss I lied on the application form. He'd probably fire me before I washed my first dish. I think I'll leave this part blank. If they ask me why, I'll say I'm going to apply for my number tomorrow.

Experience. Oh, oh. I was afraid that would be on here. "List all job experience which qualifies you for the position you're applying for." I don't have any job experience which qualifies me for the position. I don't have any job experience, period. That's the trouble with job-hunting. That's the whole trouble. You can't get a job without experience and you can't get experience until you have a job.

Would you look at that? The man in the suit is attaching a resume to his application form. A resume! He has so much experience it won't all fit in the spaces. I don't have a chance. He has a printed resume and I don't even have a Social Security number.

Oh, well. Who wants to spend eight hours a day washing dishes?

#34

What Did You Learn in School Today?

Every so often, my parents ask me the stupidest question: What did you learn in school today?

How am I supposed to answer that? I don't know what I learned. I'm sure I learned something, but it's hard to put it into a sentence or two. Usually when they ask me, I go blank and can't remember anything.

Over the years, I have learned some important facts in school, but I've never felt I should tell my parents about them. For example, school is where I learned that when girls grow up, they get hair under their arms, the same as boys, only they usually have it off. School is also where I learned the truth about Santa Claus and about the interesting photographs in some of the *National Geographic* magazines.

I never tell my folks when I learn things like that. I don't think they want to know. When they ask me what I learned in school today, they want me to say I learned the capital of Venezuela is Caracas or I learned the state bird of Nebraska is the western meadowlark. They don't want to hear that today Randy McQuire saw Miss Decker and Mr. Crumpton kissing in the back of the auditorium.

I don't tell my parents when I learn these really interesting things because I know it would upset them. I sometimes have to protect my parents from the facts of life. All kids do. We're tougher than they are and less easily shocked.

Once I decided to prepare myself for the question. I made a list of facts and carried it in my pocket, and the next time my folks said, "What did you learn in school today?" I was ready. I whipped out my list and said, "At one time, as much as twenty-seven percent of the earth's surface was covered by glacial ice. A word part added at the end of a word is called a *suffix*. Earth is ninety-three million miles from the sun. Chopin's first polonais was composed when he was eight years old. Trees that lose thei leaves are called deciduous trees. A decagon has ten angles an ten sides."

I thought they'd be pleased with such a show of knowledg but instead my dad told me not to act smart, that I should be gla they took an interest in my education.

That's the trouble with parents. They don't always mea what they say — or even what they think they mean. My folk are probably going to ask me tonight what I learned in scho today and I'm going to say, "Nothing special." The truth is, I finall learned the meaning of the word that's always written on th bathroom walls. I've wondered about that for a long time, but don't think my parents want to know.

#35

My Blankee

I am going to tell you something that I've never told anyone. still have my baby blanket.

You don't seem surprised. That's probably because you think have it packed away in a box with other keepsakes like my first eport card and my school pictures.

Wrong. I not only still have my baby blanket, I still use it. very night. Not to keep me warm, of course. Even when it was ew, it was just your normal little baby blanket, about so square, nd now it's even smaller because it's so ragged and tattered.

But The Good Place is still there — the special corner here the satin binding feels just right. Most baby blankets have Good Place, you know. Only the person who owns the blanket nows where The Good Place is, but that person can tell you exactly. he Good Place on my blanket is about this long, *(Gesture, about ix inches)* and the reason it's so good is that it feels different than he rest of the blanket. Silky. Smooth. Comforting.

When I go to bed at night, I get my blanket — actually, I've lways called it my Blankee — and I find The Good Place and hold t in my left hand. It has to be my left hand and it has to be held ust so, with my thumb on one side and the rest of my hand on he other side. Then I hold the Blankee up to my face, so I can eel it against my cheek, and I start to rub The Good Place.

I used to suck my thumb, too — the other thumb, not the ne that's rubbing The Good Place — but I don't do that anymore ecause I don't want my teeth to protrude.

Once, when I was six years old, the Tooth Fairy stole my 3lankee. She came into my room in the middle of the night and ipped me off while I was sleeping. My mother told me that the 'ooth Fairy took my Blankee when she took my first tooth because hildren who are grown up enough to lose their baby teeth no longer eed their baby blankets. I did not buy that story for one minute.

When you lose your baby teeth, it's because they aren't any good to you anymore. For days before the teeth come out, they're too loose to chew with. And no kid in his right mind would want to save an old, bloody tooth when you can put it under your pillow and get fifty cents for it. But my Blankee was not useless, like an old tooth. My Blankee was being used every single night and I knew The Good Place had plenty of years of service left.

Fortunately, the Tooth Fairy did a stupid thing. She put my Blankee on the top shelf of the linen closet. I found it a week later while my mother was at the grocery store and I was trying to find out what I was getting for my birthday. There it was, right under some scrapbooks and my mom and dad's wedding pictures.

I put it under my pillow, and that night The Good Place felt even better than I'd remembered. The next morning I took my Blankee and showed it to my mom. "Look!" I said. "The Tooth Fairy brought my Blankee back."

Mom got this funny look on her face, but she didn't say a word. She didn't even ask me why I was snooping in the linen closet. I knew she wouldn't. How could she? *She* didn't know where the Tooth Fairy put my Blankee.

#36

The Worm Farm

There's the most wonderful how-to-do-it book at the library, 1 about raising worms. Worm farming, according to the book, is 1sy! Fun! Profitable!

In the past, during my summer vacation, I've just goofed off, hich is both easy and fun, but has never been at all profitable. his year, I decided to make some money. Since I live near a lake, I gured there was a fine market for worms within walking distance ˙my house. All I would have to do is package the worms, hike over the lake, and sell them.

First I had to buy some baby worms. That's the way a worm rm works. You buy little worms, fatten them up, let them have abies, and then sell the big worms and start fattening the new ttle ones. There were several kinds to choose from and I decided ˙raise African night crawlers. They have a nice, exotic name and ie book said they grow fast, which meant I could pocket my profits ooner. I sent off my order, prepaid, for two hundred African night ˙awlers, and when they came, I dug up a big patch in my yard ˙use for a worm bed. I added a bag of steer manure because worms ke good, rich soil.

As I was spreading the steer manure around, it occurred to ie that there might be a cheaper source of supply at the farm on ie edge of town. Why pay a middleman to dry and bag a product iat I might be able to get by myself?

I rode my bike over to the farm and the farmer said he didn't ave any steers, but he had a chicken house that needed to be cleaned it. He said if I'd shovel out his chicken house, I could have everything shoveled. For free! He even gave me plastic bags to put it in.

That chicken house was not a pretty sight. When he said it eeded cleaning, he made the understatement of the year. I knew iy mother would not appreciate what I was about to do to my shoes, it a bargain's a bargain, so I waded in and started scooping. About halfway through, I took off my sweater and tied it around my face to try to keep the smell down.

When the bags were full, I hauled them home, dumped th contents on my worm bed and spread it all around on top of th steer manure. The next day, the neighbors started to complair I have to admit, the odor was not particularly pleasing, althoug all the dogs liked it just fine. They came from miles around t roll in our yard. The flies liked it, too; they buzzed and circle constantly.

I thought if I watered the worm bed, I could dilute the smel so I set up the lawn sprinkler. Besides making the smell eve stronger, this made the worms active and they all started crawlin out of the bed. I guess they thought it was raining. By the time discovered what was happening, there were worms all over th sidewalk. A flock of robins arrived and began eating them, an they must have tasted good, because the word quickly spread tha there were free African night crawlers on 31st Street, and bird of every kind started winging it to my house as fast as they could.

Meanwhile, I consulted the book and learned that I woul need to build a fence to keep the worms from crawling away whe it rained. A tin fence was recommended, one that extends severa inches into the ground.

I didn't build a fence. I didn't have any tin and I'd spent a. my money on steer manure, baby African night crawlers, and new pair of shoes, which my mother made me pay for myself.

It took me two days to turn over all the soil in the worm be so that the top layer was dirt again. That took care of the smel Then I planted some green beans in it and I had the finest bea crop in the county. Whenever anyone asked how I got my bean to grow so big, I said I spent a lot of time preparing the soil.

I sold the beans door-to-door for fifty cents a pound. It wa easy. Fun, too. And profitable — just like the book said it would b

#37

Thoughts During a Boring Sermon

There should be a law that boring sermons can only last for n minutes. Five would be even better, but ten should be maximum. I have to sit here and listen to this much longer, I'm going to fall asleep, and if I fall asleep, Mom will kill me. The trouble with having your mother sing in the choir is that she gets a perfect view of the congregation. I can never hide a magazine in my hymnal or my homework without her seeing. I can't even doodle on the offering envelope.

"Pay attention to the sermon, dear. It's good for you." Ha! How could anything this boring be good for me?

Mr. Swenson is nodding again. He does it every Sunday. About halfway through the sermon, his head starts to droop and it bobs farther and farther down until all of a sudden he jerks up again and his eyes fly open. I'm not sure if he wakes up all by himself or if Mrs. Swenson pokes him in the ribs. Then, a few minutes later, the whole process repeats itself. Bob, bob, bob — jerk! Bob, bob, bob — jerk! You *know* how dull the sermon must be if I can be fascinated by Mr. Swenson's going bob, bob, bob, jerk.

There are 218 organ pipes in this church, all of them across the back wall, behind the choir loft. There are 632 different pieces of stained glass in the picture of Mary. I counted them three Sundays in a row, to be sure I had it right. If you are interested in this kind of technical information, I can also tell you that there are forty-four horizontal pieces of wood in the altar railing and sixteen fringe balls on the cloth that covers the lectern.

I don't ever expect to need these statistics, but they give me something to think about while the sermon drones on. Drone, drone, like the steady hum of cars on a busy freeway, except there's never any screech of tires to break the monotony.

Sometimes I daydream about doing outrageous things in the middle of the sermon. I wonder what would happen if I suddenly jumped to my feet and yelled, "Anybody want to play volleyball?"

Or what if I faked a coughing attack? I could choke and gasp for breath and roll my eyes around and then get up and leave. If I hacked and coughed all the way out, I'd really raise a ruckus.

Or maybe I could pass a note around, like we sometimes do in study hall. *At exactly 11:35, everybody drop your pencil.*

What I'd really like to do is bring in one of those remote controlled toy cars and hide it under the first pew. Then, when the sermon got too boring, I'd turn it on and have it run up and down the aisle. That would wake up Mr. Swenson.

To be perfectly honest, I know I'll never do any of those things. I'm too much of a coward. I'm not afraid that God will punish me, but I'm dead certain sure my mother would. Much as I would like to rise to my feet and scream, "Fire! Fire! There's a fire in hell!" I won't ever do it. Instead, I'll pretend to pay attention to the sermon.

I wonder how many squares of ceiling tile there are in here. *(Looks up and starts to count.)* One, two, three . . .

#38

The Lemonade Stand

(The paragraphs in this scene are alternately spoken to passers-by and to yourself. Paper cups can be used as props or the actions can be pantomimed.) Lemonade! Ice-cold lemonade! Hey, mister, how 'bout a glass of lemonade? Only ten cents a glass and no charge for the ice cubes. Lemonade here. Fresh lemonade! Lemonade, missus?

(There is clearly no response. Actor shrugs and drinks a glass himself/herself.) You'd think people could at least answer me. Is it so hard to say a simple *no thanks*? Or even just a shake of the head, to let me know they heard me. But, no. I say, "Lemonade, missus?" and she looks away, quick, as if there's some sort of penalty if she's caught noticing me. It's just lemonade, for pete's sake. I'm not peddling drugs here and I'm not like those pushy people at the airport who try to get everyone to donate money. I just want to sell my lemonade before all the ice melts.

Lemonade! Ten cents for a glass of fresh, cold lemonade! *(He/she smiles broadly and holds up a glass.)* One glass, sir? Right here. *(The smile fades.)* No, I can't change a fifty. Sorry. *(He/she drinks the glass of lemonade himself/herself.)*

A fifty-dollar bill. Geez. What's he think I am, the Bank of New York? I could sell all my lemonade for a month and not make fifty bucks. I have a lemonade stand here, for pete's sake, not a savings and loan. Too bad I don't take MasterCard. I could get one of those little signs so people know they can charge it and then when someone buys my lemonade, I could get out those pieces of paper with all the carbon copies and whoosh them through the little machine. Whoosh, whoosh, sign right here, please.

*Lem*onade! *Lem*onade! Lemon*ade!* Hey, sonny, you look thirsty. Ask your mom to buy you some lemonade.

OK, OK, so don't ask her. Little brat. *(Drinks another glassful.)* *I'm* thirsty. Why isn't anyone else thirsty? I think they are;

they're just scared to buy my lemonade. They think I've put somethin' weird in it or stirred it with a dirty spoon. They think they'll get sick if they drink it and they're afraid to take the chance. They'd rather die of thirst than be poisoned by my lemonade.

Pure lemonade! No artificial ingredients! Tested for quality *(Drinks another glass and makes a show of flexing his/her muscles.)*

What I need is a gimmick. Let them think they're getting bargain. Nobody can resist a good bargain.

Half-price sale on lemonade! Regularly twenty cents glass, now only ten cents. That's right, folks. One thin dime, while the supply lasts. Lemonade sale here! Two glasses for the price one. *(Holds up a glass in each hand.)* Bring a friend. Get both glasses for just twenty cents. *(Lowers the glasses, puts one down and drinks the other.)*

No wonder so many small businesses fold each year. Everyone buys frozen lemonade at Safeway. *(He/she drinks another glass.)* What this lemonade stand needs is a bathroom. It's a wonder the Health Department hasn't shut me down.

Lemonade! Last chance to buy one and get one free!

All this yelling is sure hard on the throat. *(Drinks the last glass of lemonade.)*

Pure, fresh, cheap lemonade here! Hello, madam. Two glasses? Yes, ma'am. Coming right up. *(Looks down at the empty glasses, then back up.)* I'm sorry, ma'am. I'm all out of lemonade.

#39

All Mothers Are Clairvoyant

Did you know that all mothers are clairvoyant? It's true. There is something about having a baby which immediately endows a woman with clairvoyant powers. She is then able to perceive matters which are beyond the range of ordinary perception.

Mothers know what is going on in the next room. They know what is going on upstairs, with the door shut. They know what goes on in the school bus. My mother can even see into the future. When I wanted a dog, she said a dog would do nothing but get into trouble, and I said Skippie would never get into trouble because I would always watch him, and she said *ha,* but she let me get the dog. Then, when Skippie chewed through the cord on my electric blanket and dug up the tulip bulbs and jumped on the sofa with muddy feet, Mom kept saying, "You see? I *knew* he'd be nothing but trouble."

Mothers are so clairvoyant, they know what you do even when they're miles away. When I got home from school today, there was a chocolate layer cake in the kitchen. I knew my parents were having company tonight, so it wasn't too hard to figure out that my mother planned to serve the cake to her guests. Ordinarily, I would not take even one small piece under such circumstances. I might run my finger around the edge of the frosting a tiny bit, but I know better than to cut into a cake that my mother baked for company.

But I had forgotten to take my lunch money this morning, so I'd had nothing to eat all day. Not only that, Mrs. Franklin, my math teacher, who is fat and gross and wears knee-high pantyhose which the tops of show when she sits down, gave me a D in math, which I did not deserve, simply because I forgot to turn in my semester workbook. So when I got home and saw that chocolate cake, I couldn't help myself. I ate a piece. In fact, I ate two pieces, and having done that, I knew I had a problem. Besides having to tell my mother about the D in math, I now would have to admit I'd eaten two pieces of her chocolate cake.

For a moment, I panicked, but then I thought of a solution. I decided to take the whole cake, not just two pieces, and replace it with another one. I measured the cake, to be sure I got the right size. It was eight inches across. Then I put it on a different plate, carried it upstairs, and hid it under my bed. I planned to take it to school tomorrow and be a hero among my friends. I even toyed with the idea of giving a piece to Mrs. Franklin; maybe she'd change the D to a C-minus.

I took my entire allowance out of my bank and hustled down to the supermarket and bought a chocolate cake. I put it on the same plate that the first one had been on and set it in the same place on the kitchen counter. Now, this cake was chocolate cake with chocolate frosting, just like the other one. It measured exactly eight inches across. I figured I was home free.

When my mother got home, do you know what she said?

She said, "What did you do with my cake?" Just like that. "What did you do with my cake?"

I pointed to the cake on the counter and opened my mouth, but before I could say anything, she said, "Don't make it worse by lying to me. You ate some, didn't you, and you didn't want me to know so you went to the store and bought another one."

I could only stare at her in wonder. She was ten miles away while I was switching cakes, but she's clairvoyant, like every other mother in the world.

Since I knew I was caught, I admitted everything. Mom said she'd rather serve her homemade cake even if two pieces were missing, so I went upstairs and got down on my knees and reached under the bed.

Skippie was there. The chocolate cake wasn't.

I watched out the window until I saw Mom's guests coming up he steps. Then I told her about the D in math. I figured she wouldn't ell at me in front of company. She might not have, either, except ast as the doorbell rang, Skippie threw up on the living room rug.

I'm glad I'm not clairvoyant. I don't want to know what's oing to happen when Mom's guests leave.

#40

Christmas Surprise

This is going to be the worst Christmas of my whole life and it's all my own fault. I peeked. One day when I was home alone, went into the bedroom that used to be Marcie's before she went away to college and looked in the closet and I found my Christmas present I knew that's where it would be. And I knew Mom knew I knew and that's the worst part of all. She trusted me not to peek and peeked anyway.

I hate myself. There's just one thing I really wanted for Christmas this year. It's a panda bear, a big black and white panda and I saw him in the window of the Arthur Bird Toy Store, way back in August. I don't collect teddy bears or anything, but there was just something about that panda that made me want him. took Mom down to show her, but when she looked at the price tag she said that was pretty expensive for a bear. I said maybe Santa Claus would bring it to me and she said, "We'll see." I know who Santa Claus really is, but it's fun to pretend I don't. Mom knows know, but I think she likes pretending, too.

Some years I say I want something and then I change my mind later and want something else, but this time I never change my mind. I wanted that panda the minute I saw him and I still wanted him when it was time to write my wish list and tape it to the refrigerator. I still want him now, too, only it isn't quite the same, now that I know I'm going to get him.

How am I ever going to pretend to be surprised? Maybe should practice, to be sure I know what I'm going to say.

Oh, wow! It's the panda bear! Hooray! Hooray! I got my panda!

I wonder if that sounds too fakey. I don't want to overdo it or they'll know I peeked.

What a dope I am. I know just what's going to happen and can't stand it. Everyone will be looking at me, their eyes all shiny and loving because they know I'm going to be happy with my gift, and they'll watch me take off the ribbon and the wrapping paper and open the box and they'll be watching and smiling and excited, and then I'll have to pretend I'm surprised.

I don't think I can do it. They'll know. And if they know, it'll spoil all their fun and Christmas won't ever be the same again because they'll always wonder if I'm really surprised or if I'm just pretending.

I can't let that happen. I just can't! I'll practice being excited every day from now until Christmas, and when the time comes, I'll put on the best act in the world. I'll hug everybody and dance around the room with my panda — and I'll never, ever peek at my Christmas presents again.

#41

Mom and Dad Don't Love Each Other Anymore

You don't think it could be my fault, do you? They told me had nothing to do with it, but still, I can't help wondering. If I hadn't got into trouble by cutting through Mrs. Konen's yard all the time and if I'd kept my room clean like I was supposed to and if I'd never smarted off to them, then maybe, just maybe they'd still be together

Other kids whose parents are divorced tell me it isn't so bad, once you get used to it. You get to go to visit the parent you aren't living with, and it's kind of neat because you do special things together, just the two of you. That part sounds OK, but I'd still like it better if Dad lived at home. Maybe we didn't do a lot of special things together, just the two of us, but at least he was always here. When you see shadows outside your room at night or hear funny noises but you're too old to yell, it's comforting to know your dad's there, just down the hall.

Mom cried when she told me about the divorce, and Dad cried a little, too, when he hugged me close and said he'd see me next weekend. If they're both so sad about this, why are they doing it?

They don't love each other anymore. That's what they told me. They used to love each other, but now they don't, so they decided it would be better if they live in separate places. Better for who? Not for me, that's certain.

I wonder if they would still love each other if I'd never been born. If they hadn't had me, they would have had more money to spend on fun stuff like vacations and new cars. I'm awfully expensive. I eat quite a lot and I'm always outgrowing my clothes. Last year I fell off the monkey bars at school and chipped both my front teeth, and it cost three hundred fifty dollars to get them fixed and our insurance only paid part of it. Maybe if I didn't cost so much, Mom and Dad would still love each other.

At least they didn't make me choose between them. Before they ever told me about it, they decided that Mom and I were going to stay here and Dad was going to move out. My friend Belinda's parents made her pick between them. They told Belinda she could live with whichever one she wanted, and she was so scared that no matter who she chose, the other one would hate her for it. I don't know what I would have said. How can you pick between your mom and your dad when you love both of them?

That's the trouble, you see. They don't love each other anymore, but I still love both of them and I want everything to be like it used to be, with all of us together here in this house. How can there be Thanksgiving dinner without Dad to carve the turkey? And what about my birthday? I want them both with me on my birthday, but I can't be two places at once.

I heard Mom talking to someone on the phone. She kept saying things like, "It's really for the best," and "We tried to make it work, but we just couldn't." She sounded so cheerful, which doesn't make any sense, because I heard her crying last night, after she thought I was asleep. It's scary to hear your mom cry.

I thought when you loved somebody you loved them forever and always. That's the scariest part of all. If Mom and Dad could stop loving each other, then maybe they'll stop loving me, too. And then what will I do?

#42

You Don't Want to Buy One, Do You?

I don't know what career I'll have in the future, but I'm quite sure I won't be a salesman. I just don't seem to have the knack. No matter how well I rehearse my sales pitch, I end up saying "You really don't want to buy one, do you?" and the prospect says *no* and that's the end of it.

Unfortunately, I am the only one who is aware of this flaw in my character. Every organization I join seems to think I'll make a fine salesman and they all have a variety of items that I'm supposed to sell.

The Kid's Club had a candy sale, to raise money for new basketballs. I thought candy would be easy to sell. In fact, I thought I'd be my own best customer. I bought one box. What a ripoff! It cost me $2.25 and there were ten measly pieces of stale candy in the box. The rest was packaging. I could have bought two candy bars and been way ahead.

Once I knew what a poor bargain the candy was, it was difficult to be an enthusiastic and convincing salesman. I didn't want to gyp my friends and have them be mad at me. Even my brother, who will eat anything with sugar in it, refused to buy after he saw my box.

I finally got rid of it by knocking on doors and saying, "This is the worst candy I've ever tasted and you only get ten lousy pieces in each box, but I have to sell it if I want to be on the Kid's Club basketball team." I don't know if the customers felt sorry for me or admired my honesty, but eventually I sold all the candy.

Our school band sold magazine subscriptions. These weren't a ripoff, but a magazine subscription costs quite a lot more than a box of candy did, so it was harder to find customers. Also, the magazines we sold were not the ones which are regularly on the newsstand. I'd never heard of any of them. My mom bought a subscription to *The National Quilters Journal* and my grandpa bought one called *Rock Collecting for Seniors,* but that was it. That's all I sold — two magazine subscriptions. The band director gave an award for best salesman, but I didn't get it.

Once I had to stand in front of the Safeway and try to sell raffle tickets. People acted like I had a communicable disease or something. I stood there by the automatic doors and watched people approach from the parking lot. I could always tell when they noticed me. Some people would immediately look down at the ground and they'd keep staring at the ground until they were past me. Others would turn their heads and look away from me. A few would speed up, as if trying to tell me they were in a terrible hurry and didn't have time to see what I was selling. One woman opened her purse and dug around in it like she was looking for something. As soon as she passed me, she closed her purse.

Standing in front of Safeway is still better than knocking on doors. I hate selling things door-to-door. The people who know me get embarrassed because it's hard to say *no* to the neighbor kid, and besides, they don't want to seem cheap. The people who don't know me are annoyed because I interrupted them when they were watching the football game or washing dishes or whatever they were doing. Nobody is glad to see me and nobody's anxious to buy.

I know I won't be a salesman when I'm grown, but I hope I make lots of money in whatever job I have. Then, when I see a kid standing in front of Safeway with raffle tickets or boxes of candy, I'll walk right up to him, look him in the eye and say, "I'll take two."

#43

The Bald Eagle

One day as David and I drove down Lakeside Boulevard, I happened to look up in the trees and there, sitting way at the top, was a bald eagle. A bald eagle, right there on Lakeside Boulevard! I yelled for David to stop the car, and he did, and we got out and walked back to where we could see the eagle better. I wish I'd had my binoculars, but even without them, I got a good look at him. His head and tail were white and the rest of his body was brown, and he had a large, curved beak. He looked so — majestic seems trite, but that's the only appropriate word — he looked majestic sitting on the branch of that alder tree.

Cars sped past us in both directions, but none of them stopped. The drivers didn't even slow down to see what we were staring at. Wouldn't you think they'd be curious about why we were standing on the side of the road, gazing up into the trees? I wanted to yell at them: "Hey, all you people! You are passing a bald eagle! You're in such a hurry to get to work or the grocery store or wherever you are going, you're missing your chance to see a real, live bald eagle. An endangered species. Our national bird!" I didn't yell, of course, and nobody else stopped.

Neither David nor I ever saw an eagle out of captivity before. The only one I'd ever seen was in one of those wildlife parks where you ride through on a little tram and see the animals in what is supposed to be their natural habitat but which is really just a form of captivity.

This eagle was free. He sat there in the top of the tree for another three or four minutes and then he lifted off and flew across the lake, his huge wings flapping slowly as he sailed high above the water. David and I watched him go until he got so small we couldn't see him anymore.

Neither of us said anything. We just watched the bald eagle fly away and then we walked back to the car and got in and drove off. What could we have said to each other? Wasn't he beautiful? Wasn't he big? Words. There were no words that morning to describe what we had seen, and we both knew better than to try.

Somehow, seeing the bald eagle made me feel patriotic — and it also gave me hope. In a world filled with terrorists and senseless killings, there are still opportunities to see a bald eagle, flying free.

#44

Cafeteria Lunches

Have you ever noticed that very few kids are fat? People don't start to get pudgy until they grow up and finish school. There is a logical reason for this and it has nothing to do with age. Kids don't get fat because they have to eat lunch in the school cafeteria every day, and the cafeteria lunches are so bad that we eat only enough to keep from starving and not one bite more.

My school cafeteria serves the most gross things you can imagine. And they aren't even honest about it. They try to camouflage these nonfoods by calling them by fancy names. Every Friday the menu for the next week's lunches is published. That way you can bring a bag lunch if there's a day when the cafeteria is serving something you're allergic to or don't like. The tricky part is figuring out what the menus mean.

Whoever writes the menus tries to trick us into thinking the food is exciting. During football season, the cafeteria serves things like Touchdown Casserole. That may be a catchy name, but it doesn't give a clue as to what's in the casserole. Is it hamburger or tuna? Macaroni or asparagus? I like to know what to expect so I can get psyched up for it.

Once we had something called Strawberry Dreams. It sounded quite tasty. I imagined Strawberry Dreams would consist of a buttery cookie crust and a filling of fresh strawberries and maybe some crushed pineapple, all topped with a big spoonful of whipped cream. The Strawberry Dreams turned out to be dishes of runny custard with a glob of strawberry jam on top. They should have been called Strawberry Nightmares.

The menu writer really comes into her own when there's a holiday. For Halloween we got Witches' Brew Hot Dish, Goblin Salad, Jack-o-Lantern Bread and Black Cat Cookies.

Valentine's Day was even worse. That day the menu was Love Boat Soup, Cupid Crackers, Heart Sandwiches and Hugs 'n Kisses Cake. Heart Sandwiches? Yuck! I wouldn't even take a taste

If we students had our way, we'd all bring a bag lunch every day and there would be no need for a cafeteria. But many parents — mine included — insist that their kids buy lunch at school every day. They say they want us to have a well-balanced hot meal. The truth is, they don't want to bother with sandwich meats and other lunch ingredients when they shop for groceries.

The worst cafeteria days of all are those called Cook's Choice. You might expect Cook's Choice to be the cook's most favorite recipes, something particularly tasty. Wrong. Cook's Choice means there are a bunch of leftover ingredients which need to be used up before they spoil, and so the cook has put them all together into a horrible concoction which nobody can recognize and which is unfit for human consumption. If it is possible to avoid eating in the cafeteria on Cook's Choice day, I advise you to do so.

If you can't bring your lunch to school and have no alternative but to eat in the cafeteria, at least you can take comfort in knowing you aren't likely to get fat. Not when you're served Hockey Puck Cookies for dessert.

#45

There's a Golf Ball in that Tree

I live near a golf course. I don't play golf because I don't have any golf clubs, but I like to go for walks on the golf course in the evening when most of the golfers have gone home. There are lots of trees and green grass and a little stream that crisscrosses back and forth. In the summer, I pick wild blackberries from the bushes that grow along the golf course fence.

I find a lot of golf balls on my walks, especially on the stream banks and in the berry bushes. At first I didn't know what to do with them. Golf balls really aren't good for much except playing golf. Then I got the idea of hiding the golf balls and seeing how long it takes before someone finds them. I carry a notebook with me on my walks. When I hide a golf ball, I write down the date and where I hid it and then, each time I go for a walk, I check to see if the ball has been found yet.

I've hidden golf balls on the railings of the little bridges that cross the stream and I've put them underneath the benches where people sit while they're waiting to tee off. My favorite hiding places are in the trees. Not on the ground underneath the trees — *in* the trees. I'll put a shiny white golf ball in the crook of a tree, right where a branch meets the trunk. Usually, it's plainly visible — if anyone was looking for a golf ball in a tree. They aren't, of course. People who hit their balls into the trees go looking for them with their eyes on the ground. One ball stayed in the same tree for twenty-seven days. That's my record, so far. Twenty-seven days without being found. Usually someone finds the balls in less than a week, especially if the weather's nice and lots of people are out playing golf.

I've always wished I could be there when one of my balls is discovered. I like to imagine that the person gets all excited and calls out, "Hey, look at this! There's a golf ball in that tree! Isn't that crazy?" And then everyone laughs and when they get home, they tell their families how they found a golf ball stuck in a tree.

The people who originally lost the balls were probably unhappy about it. I hope one of them finds a golf ball in a tree someday.

#46

How I Almost Made
One Thousand Dollars

Last summer I decided to get a Real Job. I was sick of baby-sitting and mowing lawns and taking care of our neighbor's dogs. I was ready to earn some Big Bucks.

I answered all the ads in the newspaper, but the employers were mostly hiring college kids or people with some experience. I didn't stand a chance.

Then I saw an ad that said, "No experience necessary. We train. Make big money selling what every household needs." I called the number in the ad and was given an appointment for an interview.

It turned out to be a group interview and everyone who showed up got hired. We were going to sell zip code directories, and each person was assigned a different part of town so we wouldn't compete with each other. Harold, the man who hired us, was really excited about zip code directories. He told about going into one business office and selling forty-five directories, just like that. He made sixty-seven dollars for only ten minutes' work!

By the time the meeting ended, I was convinced I could make a thousand dollars a month by selling zip code directories, and I could hardly wait to begin. There was just one catch. We had to pay for the directories before we could take them with us. Each directory cost two dollars and we were supposed to sell them for $3.50. That's a pretty good profit, and from the way Harold talked, it was going to be a snap to get rid of them. I said I'd take one hundred directories to start but I'd probably be back for more by the end of the week.

When I told my mother I needed a check for two hundred dollars in order to begin my new job, she said to forget it. I couldn't believe my ears! My own mother, who is always telling me if I want to get ahead in the world I have to do something besides watch TV, was refusing to help me get started in my new job. After a great deal of discussion, she finally agreed to give me twenty dollars. I got my ten zip code directories and started out on my route.

At the end of the first day, I'd sold none. I knocked on twenty-seven doors and made zero sales. The second day, I sold one — to my grandmother. The third day, I decided to forget my assigned route and go to some office buildings. If Harold could sell forty-five directories in one place, maybe I'd get lucky, too. Wrong. Half the businesses had rules about no soliciting, and the other half didn't need zip code directories.

By then I was plenty discouraged. I went home and asked my mother if she wanted to buy a zip code directory and she said it appeared to her that she already owned nine of them at a cost of two dollars each. I couldn't argue with that, but it made me mad, so I left and went around my neighborhood. I called on all the people who could always be counted on to purchase raffle tickets for the school or candy for the Scouts.

It took several hours because people asked me a lot of questions like who got to keep the money. I discovered sales are easier to make if the money goes to the Scouts than if it's going in my pocket. Only two neighbors bought zip code directories from me. That was it. I never sold another zip code directory. Not only did I fail to make one thousand dollars, my mother made me pay her back the twenty.

#47

My Mother Collects China Cows

My mother collects china cows. She has all these little cream pitchers that look like cows. Anyone who wants cream in his coffee at our house has to pick up a little china cow, hold it by the tail and tip it forward. It always looks like the cow is throwing up into the person's coffee, which isn't exactly appetizing, but that's the only way my mother will serve cream. She has thirty-eight china cows to choose from, so they get to take turns throwing up. She uses the bigger cow pitchers for maple syrup when we have pancakes, and the syrup looks just as gross coming out of the cow's mouth as the cream does.

My friend's mother collects frogs. Not real frogs. She collects glass frogs, pottery frogs, frogs of every kind and size. The scale in her bathroom looks like a frog, and there are about a dozen different ceramic and plastic frogs lined up on the kitchen window sill.

A frog is not a creature of beauty. Its eyes bulge out of its head, its back legs are too long and its body is anything but graceful. Why would anyone want to live with a bunch of frogs?

I don't understand why mature adults surround themselves with such silly collections. All those cows and frogs cost a lot of money, they're a nuisance to dust, and they don't appreciate in value. It doesn't make any sense at all.

These aren't isolated instances, either. One man saves pieces of different kinds of barbed wire. He hangs them on his walls. His living room looks like a concentration camp.

Quite a few people collect teddy bears. As a result, teddy bears are expensive. If you're going to have a collection, you should collect something that nobody else wants. That way it won't cost so much.

One woman collects salt and pepper shakers. Did you ever hear of anything so foolish? One salt shaker and one pepper shaker ught to be plenty for anyone, but she has one set that looks like lackbirds and one set that looks like little tulips. She even has a et where the salt shaker is a ghost and the pepper shaker is a ombstone. I suppose she uses them on Halloween. Or maybe she oesn't use them at all. That's something I've noticed about people ith collections. They don't necessarily *use* the items they collect. Iostly, the things just sit on shelves, gathering dust.

I could go on. I could tell you about the crazy people who ollect marbles and license plates and baskets. But I have to go ow and straighten up my room. My mother, the woman with hirty-eight china cows, says if I don't put away all my old comic ooks and my *(Name of popular singer)* posters, she's going to hrow them out.

#48

The Cat Door

My dad installed a cat door in our house. The cat door is little metal flap that swings both ways so our cat, Prudence, ca let herself in and out. The purpose of the cat door was to keep Prudenc from playing the piano in the middle of the night, which is wha she does when she wants to go out and everyone is asleep.

With the addition of our cat door, Prudence could go in an out whenever she wanted, even if no one was home. This prove to be a mixed blessing. It put an end to Prudence's midnight pian recitals, but it also subjected our family to the trauma of tail-les lizards.

We live in a hot, dry climate where there are many littl lizards. Prudence likes to catch them. She sometimes catches mic too, but when she catches a mouse, she eats it. All of it. When sh catches a lizard, she only eats the tail. I guess the tail is the onl part of a lizard that tastes good. Strangely enough, the lizard don't seem to mind. They just go on about their business, lackin a tail.

Ever since she got her cat door, Prudence has been bringin the lizards inside. Then she eats the tail and the rest of the lizar skitters away, looking for a dark place to hide. There are som dandy dark hiding places in our house.

My dad's shoe was one. He stuck his foot in his shoe, let ou a yell, pulled the shoe off, and turned it over. A tail-less lizard fel to the floor. Another time, my mother sat down on the couch an reached for the wicker basket where she keeps her knitting. As sh picked up the yarn and the sweater she was making, a tail-les lizard dropped out onto her lap.

When Prudence isn't catching lizards, she likes to figh One night there was a cat fight in our living room. I don't know Prudence ran home and the other cat followed her or if the othe cat discovered the cat door on its own and decided to investigate was awakened at two a.m. by the worst commotion I'd ever heard. cat fight is unlike any other sound. They screech at each other. hey hiss. They make a low, gutteral sound that erupts suddenly ito a piercing shriek.

That night, Prudence and her visitor were on top of the rown chair, screaming and clawing at each other, and Dad, who ad rushed downstairs in his pajamas, was clapping his hands and elling at them to be quiet. I got there just in time to see a black tail isappear through the cat door. Dad quickly flipped the little lock hich prevents the door from opening. When I asked him what e was doing, he said he was making sure the other cat didn't me back in. Dad didn't have his glasses on. He was surprised hen I pointed out that it was Prudence who had streaked out ie cat door. The other cat was prowling around our living room, antically trying to escape.

Eventually, we chased the other cat out the front door. Then e unlocked the cat door so Prudence could come back home when ie was ready. She came the next morning and she brought a eace offering. Mom was fixing breakfast when Prudence came ito the kitchen and rubbed against Mom's ankles. Mom leaned wn absent-mindedly to pet Prudence, and that's when she saw ie snake. It was coiled on the kitchen floor where Prudence had ropped it, and its tongue was darting in and out.

We don't have a cat door anymore. Not only is it fastened iut, there's a board nailed across it.

#49

Six Snickers, Four Candy Corn and Three Purple Bubblegum

There's a special feeling in the air on Halloween night. A up and down the street, porch lights shine and jack-o-lantern glow. Kids dressed like goblins and witches and black cats scurr eagerly from house to house, laughing and shouting. Pirates an gypsies pass each other on the sidewalk and exchange informatio about which houses are passing out the best treats.

Halloween is my most favorite holiday, even though w have to go to school. Even school is fun, on Halloween. I hope th government never decides to change Halloween and make it be th last Monday in October just so a lot of people can have a long weekend Halloween should stay just the way it is.

Planning a costume is the first step. Some of my costume have been really great — like the year my friend and I went togethe and were Harvey, the giant rabbit. My friend was the front en and wore big ears and whiskers; I was the back end and wore a ta made out of cotton. We made the rabbit suit out of an old shee and we bunny-hopped all over school that year. I couldn't se where we were going, but it didn't matter. I could hear everyon laughing.

Carving the pumpkin is another part of Halloween that fun. I always put eyelashes on mine, and big, jagged teeth.

But the best part is going out for trick or treat. I go wit my brother and the kids next door, and our parents make us wa until it's dark out. Then we get a lecture: only go to houses whe the porch light is on; be sure to say *thank you;* don't eat anythin that isn't wrapped; and be careful crossing the street. We don listen to the lecture because we're mentally planning our rout We've heard it all before, anyway.

Finally, like horses at the starting gate, we are release and we bolt out the door.

Most of the adults who answer our knocks are smiling. They admire the costumes or try to guess who it is as they dole out the treats.

Afterwards, when I get back home, I sort out my loot and count it. I dump everything from my trick or treat bag onto the floor and separate it into little piles. Six Snickers bars, four bags of candy corn, three pieces of purple bubblegum, five Almond Joys, three Goo-Goo Clusters and one full-size Hershey bar. Not bite-size, like all the others, but a genuine full-size Hershey bar. Bless you, Mrs. Munson; may you live for many more Halloweens.

There are always a couple of boxes of raisins, too, from people who are conscious of good nutrition and object to the consumption of so much sugar. I understand their point of view and appreciate their concern for my health, but, believe me, those aren't the houses which are mentioned when the ghosts and ghoulies pause to tell each other where to get the best goodies. I always eat the raisins last, after everything else is gone.

My mother, who has a sweet tooth, used to try to sneak some candy from my bag after I went to bed, but I always found out. I *now* whether there are five Snickers bars left or only four. Even my little brother, who isn't too bright sometimes, knows exactly how many of each kind he has. Mom can't sneak anything from him, either, so instead of stealing, she begs.

She'll watch us counting our piles, and pretty soon she won't be able to stand it, and she'll ask if she can have one. I always try to give her a box of raisins, but eventually, I give in and let her have a candy bar or two. On Halloween, I can afford to be generous.

#50

The Driver's Test
Is a Piece of Cake

My brother said there's nothing to it; the driver's test is a piece of cake. That's easy for him to say. He got his license three years ago.

I didn't expect to be quite this nervous. I took Driver's Training. I even got an A. I studied the manual and passed the written test and got my permit. I've been creating reasons to drive for six months, to get lots of practice. So why should I be nervous, just because I'm going to take the driving test? If I flunk it, I can always take it over. Oh, Lord, if I flunk it, I'll die. Everyone knows I'm taking the test today. I don't think I could stand it if I flunked.

I just hope I don't throw up in the middle of it. I shouldn't have eaten anything for breakfast. If I get sick in the middle of the driving test, I'll flunk for sure.

Here comes the examiner. What a mean-looking man. He won't even smile at me. I'll bet he marks me down for every little thing. He probably has a prejudice against teenage drivers.

Well, here goes. Start the engine. What if it doesn't start? What if I flood it? I'll fail the test before I even get out of the parking lot.

There. There, it started. All right now. Look in the mirror before I back up. Shift into forward. Turn on the signal. Why is he looking at me like that? Did I do something wrong already? What is he writing on that paper? I *am* going to throw up; I can feel it coming.

Oh, good, a break in the traffic. I can finally go.

All right. It shouldn't be too bad now, just driving down the street.

Around the block. Signal, look both ways, turn into the back side of the parking lot. Oh, no! I have to parallel park between those two red markers. But they're so short. When I practiced parallel parking, it was between two cars. You can see cars; you can't see those little markers. I wonder if he'd let me skip this part if I swear that for the rest of my life I'll drive around until I find a parking place on the corner.

Probably not. Probably, he'd say . . . oh, Lord, I hit one of the markers. Oh, I wish I could die. Now I have to start all over again. I hit it but I didn't knock it over, so I get a second chance. Around the block, signal, look both ways, stay in the proper lane.

I'm sweating. I can feel it running down my arms. I'm going to ruin my good sweater just because of those stupid red markers.

There! I did it! I parked and I didn't hit either one of them. I got *out* of the space without hitting them, too.

Back to the starting gate and stop the engine. That's it. My driver's test is over. He's handing me the paper. Eighty-four. I got eighty-four! I passed! I get my license.

Well, that wasn't so bad, after all. I'll tell my friends that my brother was right. Taking the driver's test is nothing. A piece of cake.

#51

There's Nothing to Do Around Here

There is absolutely nothing to do around here. I live in the most boring house in the whole universe. Day after day, it's the same old things. When I complain that there's nothing to do, my mom always suggests dumb stuff like, "Why don't you read a book?" or "Why don't you work a jigsaw puzzle?"

I've read all my books. Well, maybe not all of them, but I've read all the ones I feel like reading, and it's too much effort to go to the library. And I'm sick of working jigsaw puzzles. I already worked one in June, during the first week of school vacation, and that was enough.

My dad's no help, either. If I tell him there's nothing to do, he always says if I want something to do, I can mow the grass or wash a few windows.

You should see my room. It is so dull. If there were a world record for dull rooms, my room would be the winner. There's a big shelf filled with books and a lot of old games and toys — stuff from my birthday that I've been sick of for months. There's a toy chest, too, and the things in there are even worse. I bet some of those toys have been in that chest since I was a baby. I outgrew Candyland years ago, but it's still there, and I bet if my mom saw it, she would suggest I invite a friend over to play Candyland with me. I'd die of embarrassment.

We have this stupid rule at our house that you can't watch television before five o'clock, unless you're sick. The rule is supposed to keep me from filling my mind with junk programs. The theory is that I will do constructive activities instead of sitting around like a blob. The theory might work if there was something else to do around here, but there isn't.

Yesterday I was rooting around for something — anything — to do and I found a half-empty bottle of soap bubble solution.

aven't played with soap bubbles for years, but I took the cap off
nd blew a few bubbles, just to see if the solution was any good. Mom
ad a fit; she said the soap would leave rings on the furniture, and
' I wanted to blow bubbles, I could go outside. But it was hot
ut and I was comfy on the floor, and I didn't really want to blow
ubbles anyway. Bubble-blowing is too babyish.

I'd ride my bike except there's nowhere to go. Mom said I
uld bake cookies, but we're out of chocolate chips, and that's the
nly kind that sounds good. I don't feel like listening to records,
nd there's no one to play ball with, and if I get out my paint set,
ll make a mess and have to clean it up.

What I really want to do is go to the movies, but I've already
ent all my allowance this week and my parents won't give me any
ore. They said I'll just have to entertain myself until Saturday,
hich is when I get my next allowance.

I don't mind entertaining myself. I'd be glad to entertain
yself, if I had something to entertain myself with. But there is
othing. I am stuck for the rest of the summer in the world's dullest
ouse, where there is absolutely nothing to do.

#52

Dogs, Orion and Buttons

In the past year, I've learned to like dogs, Orion and buttons. It isn't that I *dis*liked those things before; I just didn't pay any attention to them, one way or another.

Until this year, I never had a dog. I never spent any time with a dog. I never knew any dogs personally and I thought a dog was a pet the way a goldfish is a pet. Then last summer my brother begged until he got a puppy, and from the moment Pepper became a part of our household, I realized how much I'd been missing.

Pepper has plenty of puppy love for all of us and he gives it unconditionally. In all the months he's lived with us, Pepper has never been angry at me. He is always sad when I leave and overjoyed when I return. If I want to play with him, he's delighted to run and fetch. It is never too early or too late for a fine game of slobber-ball and he is never too busy or too tired to accompany me on a walk. Pepper doesn't care if I'm thin or fat, short or tall, ugly or beautiful.

When I meet other dogs now, I always pet them. I laugh when I see a dog wearing a bandana or a raincoat and I talk to its owner and ask how old the dog is. Loving Pepper has changed me. I like dogs! But if we hadn't adopted Pepper, I wouldn't know I like dogs.

I wouldn't know I like Orion, either, if I hadn't been required to take one unit of astronomy as part of my science class. Each of us had to write a report on a constellation and I chose Orion. I learned that Orion was a great hunter, and after his death, he was placed among the stars. I learned how to find his belt and the three diagonal stars which form his sword. I used to look up at the sky and see only stars. Now I also see Orion.

As for buttons, I always thought they were strictly functional, a way to keep my clothing fastened. Then our neighbor showed me her button collection and told me about some of the older and more interesting buttons. She has buttons made of ivory and glass and

other-of-pearl. There are buttons shaped like tiny vegetables
nd brass buttons from old military uniforms. One of her buttons
worth three hundred dollars!

Ever since that day, I've noticed what kind of buttons people
ear. Once, a clerk in the drugstore had a copper eagle button on
er jacket, and when I mentioned it, she told me the button was a
eorge Washington Inaugural Button. She said the buttons were
ade as souvenirs of George Washington's inaugurations, and her
reat-grandmother got one.

I wonder how many other people talked to the clerk that
ay but never noticed the George Washington Inaugural Button.
wonder what else *I'm* missing. Until this year, I'd looked at the
ars hundreds of times and never saw Orion. And there's no telling
ow many cute, friendly dogs I've walked past without noticing
em.

What am I passing still, unseeing and unknowing? What
m I missing because I lack the knowledge or experience to notice?

#53

Long, Hot Showers

When athletes are kicked out of a game, they are sent to th showers. It is not a fate they desire. Other people who get in troubl are said to be in hot water. This is not a compliment, either. Frankly I don't understand why either of those phrases is used in such derogatory way.

I love hot showers. Long, hot showers. Nothing feels bette than to stand in the shower with the hot water beating down on m shoulders and the steam rising up to make the mirror all foggy.

I like to shampoo my hair in the shower. I put my head unde the spigot and squeeze my eyes shut tight and put my fingers i my ears and let the water pour over my face. Then I turn aroun lean my head back, and let the water stream down the other way I work the shampoo into my hair until it's thick and sudsy, an when I rinse it off, great gobs of white foam slither down m arms and drop off my elbows.

Whenever I have a head cold, a long hot shower makes m feel better. Breathing in all that steam clears up my nose.

If I'm worried about something, a shower makes me fee better, too. Some people like to meditate and some people li weights and some people run. I take a long, hot shower, and whe I'm finished, my problems never seem as big as they did befor

A hot shower sometimes creates a different problem, thoug My parents have been known to bang on the bathroom door an yell about how high the electric bill was last month. They don understand that a long, hot shower is not just a way to get clea It's also good therapy. How could I be unhappy when hot water i streaming across my face and the whole bathroom feels like a saun

If I ever get in trouble, I'll be glad if I'm sent to the shower Being in hot water is just fine with me.

#54

The Last Day of Sixth Grade

Yesterday was the last day of school. That is, it was my last day in the sixth grade. It won't really be the last day of school for me until I graduate, on the last day of twelfth grade. Or, if I decide to go to college, the last day of school will be the last day of xteenth grade. If I decide to be a doctor, the last day will come at the end of twenty-second grade. Yuck! Can you imagine anyone going to school for twenty-two years? I've barely been able to stand for seven, and that includes kindergarten, where all we did was color pictures, sing songs and memorize our telephone numbers.

Anyway, yesterday was the last day of sixth grade, and I thought the hands of the clock would never get around to 3:08. That's what time our school gets out. 3:08. Not three o'clock, which would be a sensible number, or even 3:15, which at least has a definite place on most watches. Nope. 3:08. Someday I'm going to demand an explanation for that. Probably the reason is because school starts each morning at 7:52 and the principal wants the school day to have an even seven hours. That may not sound logical, but a lot of things at Woodhill School are not logical.

To prove my point, I will tell you what we did on the last day of sixth grade. I know you'll find this hard to believe, because the last day of school is supposed to be spent having parties and cleaning nine months' worth of moldy sandwich crusts out of lockers and talking about what we're going to do during summer vacation.

Not in Miss Millard's class. In Miss Millard's class, where I unfortunately, was captive, we gave oral reports. Can you believe it? Oral reports on the last day of school!

Most of the reports were just plain stupid. You would think by the time people have made it all the way through sixth grade, they would think of something imaginative to talk about. The topic was "The Most Interesting Thing That's Happened This Year," and from the way those reports went, it was a pretty dull year at Woodhill School.

Karen Craigmeyer actually reported on a movie we saw one day in English class. How boring can you be? We all saw the same movie. Personally, I think Karen Craigmeyer was worried that she might flunk sixth grade and she was trying to impress Miss Millard.

I gave my report on "The Worst Nightmare I Ever Had." It was all about how I climbed up in the attic of my house and crawled along the rafters and slipped and fell through the living room ceiling. I landed on top of my brother's piano teacher, and she fell off the piano bench and broke her back. The piano teacher screamed in agony and my brother started crying and my mother ran to call an ambulance.

When I got to the part about the ambulance coming to our house with the siren going and its lights flashing, I had the whole sixth-grade class sitting forward in its chairs. And when the medics slipped on the icy sidewalk and dropped the piano teacher into a snowbank, broken back and all, the entire class gasped with shock.

Actually, I made the whole thing up. I hardly ever have nightmares. But I got an A on my report — and I got through the last day of sixth grade.

#55

On Being Different

It isn't easy to be different from the other kids. I don't mean different because of skin color or different because of how much money your family has. I mean different inside, a way of thinking and looking at the world which isn't the same as most other people.

At first I didn't know I was different; I thought everybody was like me. When I started school, I realized this isn't true. Most people are like each other, but they aren't like me.

It is glorious to be the exception to the rule; it is also very painful. Sometimes I wish I could be like everyone else. I want to like what they like and do what they do and feel as they feel. Except when they get hysterical over some singer and then I'm glad I'm different. Why should someone be worshipped just because he can sing?

My differentness ranges from God to deodorants, with a good many things in between. Most of my friends believe in God. Some of them even claim to know Jesus Christ personally. Because of this acquaintance, they know what is right and what is wrong and exactly how they and everyone else is supposed to behave. I envy them their certainty. I have read about God and about Jesus. I've also read about Buddha and about humanism and about the similarities between all the world's great religions. I'm still unsure what is right and what is wrong on some issues. I try to be kind and moral, but sometimes I'm plagued with doubts and questions. It would be so much easier to know.

As for deodorant, I find that if I wash under my arms every day, I don't need one, no matter what the advertisers claim. I have also discovered it is unwise to make such a statement to one's peers.

It isn't that I'm smarter than the others; I'm just different. Sometimes I wonder if I lack some vital chromosome. I am bored by things which interest other people and interested in things which other people never notice. I don't know the names of any of

the new cars or which movies have been nominated for Oscars thi
year or what albums have sold a million copies. I do know tha
when my cat is close enough to me to feel secure, her tail goes up i
the air, and when I move away from her, her tail points down.
find this fascinating — a comment on cats in general, my cat i
particular, and even an insight into the whole relationship betwee
love and trust. I get great pleasure from seeing my cat's tail g
from *down* to *up* as she approaches me. When I mentioned this a
school, the other kids looked at me like I was a freak.

When I first realized I was different, I tried to change.
pretended to like what everyone else liked. I still do this occasionally
but it has never worked very well. When all the kids began watchin,
(Name of popular TV show) every week, I watched it, too, so
wouldn't feel left out the next morning when they discussed it
Unfortunately, I discovered I don't much like *(Name of TV show,*
I never admitted that to my friends, though. When you're different
you learn to keep your mouth shut.

Because I'm different, I never quite belong. Oh, I have friends
but I know I'm not really like them, and they know it, too. And n
matter how much we talk or how many activities we do together
we will never be alike. I remain the exception to the rule.

Since I can't change what I am, I've decided to accept it
It's been easier to do this since I met Nancy. We'd known each othe
only a few days when she told me she wasn't like the rest of th
kids. She confided that she doesn't even watch *(Name of TV show,*
She wasn't apologizing; she was stating a fact.

When Nancy told me she was different, I looked at he
and smiled. If I were a cat, my tail would have gone straight up i
the air.

#56

Inventions I Intend to Make

Someday, when I don't have to go to school anymore and therefore have lots of free time, I'm going to be an inventor. There are a number of inventions which I've already thought of that I plan to build. For example, a machine that makes yarn out of pet fur. Every day, thousands of people brush and comb their household pets. All across the land, dogs and cats of every variety are being groomed — but what happens to the fur which is removed? It's discarded. It's plucked out of combs and brushes and thrown in the trash can. What a waste of a fine natural resource.

If there were a machine which could spin all of that excess fur into yarn, the yarn could be used to knit sweaters, mittens, socks — maybe even pet-fur coats. People who love collies could wear collie-fur mittens. People who prefer Siamese cats could buy Siamese-fur sweaters. There could be a Pet-Fur Recycling Center in every city where people could drop off their bags of dog and cat combings. It's such a great idea, I'm surprised it hasn't been done already.

One invention that I know will be successful is my Detachable Floor Scrubber. Each Detachable Floor Scrubber is going to be a small brush which moves from side to side, followed by a sponge. They'll be hooked to a metal clamp that attaches to the sides of any pair of shoes, much like a spur.

A supply of Detachable Floor Scrubbers can be kept just outside the door of your home, along with a bucket of soapy water. When you come home, you dip the brush in the bucket and then clamp the Floor Scrubber on the side of your foot, using one for each shoe. Then you can walk in the house and each time you take a step, the soapy brush moves back and forth behind your shoe, and the sponge drags along behind the brush to soak up the water and dirt. No floor will ever be dirty again — and no kid will ever get yelled at for tracking in mud.

Probably my best invention idea is my Automatic Food-Finder. This device will be particularly useful for children in large families because the mothers in such families tend to hide food in strange places. I know. I have six brothers, and my mother hides food all the time. She has even been known to keep cookies in her mending basket.

Usually she does it because she's promised to bake something for a school function or a church bazaar and she's afraid we'll eat it before she can leave the house. There is good reason for this fear, which is based on long and practical experience. My feeling is, why should the PTA or the church take priority over starving children?

And that's why I plan to invent my Automatic Food-Finder. My device will be hand-held and you will be able to run it along the kitchen cupboards, appliances, broom closets, desk drawers and other places where food might be stashed away. When it comes within two feet of food, lights will flash. I thought of having a bell ring, too, but I decided it might be better to remain quiet and not call unnecessary attention to the fact that an Automatic Food-Finder is in use.

If I'd had this invention last week, it would have saved my mother a lot of trouble. She baked two dozen chocolate cupcakes to take to a Teacher's Tea at my oldest brother's school. When the cupcakes were frosted, she carefully placed them in the bottom of the washing machine. She was sure that none of us would do a load of laundry without being commanded to do so. The next morning, which was the day of the Teacher's Tea, Mother went out to the kitchen and did all of the things she habitually does first thing in the morning. She started a pot of coffee, began packing school lunches, and flipped on the washing machine so it would begin to fill. When she opened the lid to put in the dirty clothes, she remembered the Teacher's Tea; twenty-four soggy cupcakes were floating around in the water.

It never would have happened if I'd had my Automatic Food-Finder. Those cupcakes would never have stayed in the washer overnight.

#57

Precious Keepsakes

No! I'm not going!

I don't care if everyone else in the family is going to be there. I don't care if everyone else in the entire state of California is going to be there. I am not going and that's final. I refuse to be a part of this money-grabbing selfishness.

Where were all these people, all these relatives and so-called "dear" friends, when Grandpa was so sick? Where were they then, when he would have welcomed some company, a chance to sit and talk about the old days or play a game of checkers? Did anyone show up then, when it would have done some good?

Oh, no. They were all too busy. Everyone was working and too tired after work to go see Grandpa. Well, nobody seems to be too busy or too tired to attend a meeting about how to divide up Grandpa's personal property. Everyone got time off work today with no trouble.

I think it stinks! Talk about a bunch of hypocrites. Everyone saying things like, "It's hard to do, but of course we have to do it." Wrong! They don't have to do it. They want to do it. Everyone wants to come and be sure he gets his fair share. If you want my opinion, their fair share is nothing. Zippo. They should sell it all and give the money to the Salvation Army. Buy food for the needy. They won't, though. They'll argue and bicker over every little thing. They'll probably fight about who gets the box of paper clips on Grandpa's desk.

It's the squabbling I can't stand. "I'd like to have Grandpa's old watch." "Oh, I'm sorry, he promised that to me." "I hate to disagree with you, but he told me years ago that the gold watch would be mine someday."

It makes me sick. I wish they'd buried the gold watch with Grandpa.

Can't they see how they're acting? Don't they hear how they sound? It's like a flock of crows, cawing and fighting over bit of discarded food.

Well, this little bird is having no part of it. If I want something to remember Grandpa by, all I have to do is look at one of my snapshots or close my eyes and picture how he looked when he sat across from me, playing checkers. That's my keepsake and it's better than all the gold watches ever made.

#58

The World's Greatest Tinfoil Collection

My road to fame began in an unlikely place — the shoe department of Underwood's Clothing Store. That's where I saw the biggest ball of rubber bands in the world. It was more than twelve inches in diameter.

The shoe clerk made it. Each pair of shoes comes in a shoe box with a rubber band around it, and one day, the clerk wound a rubber band around and around until it was a little ball and then he opened another box and wound the next rubber band around the first one. From then on, every time he opened a new box of shoes, he added another rubber band and the ball got bigger and bigger. Pretty soon it was a real challenge to keep the rubber bands from breaking as he stretched them around the existing ball.

That clerk expects to have his name and a picture of his rubber-band ball in the next edition of the *Guinness Book of World Records*.

I thought about the ball of rubber bands all the way home and I decided that I would do what that shoe clerk did. Not with rubber bands, of course. That wouldn't be original. I mean, I decided to do something all my own that would result in *my* having the biggest of something. The biggest in the entire world, and I'd get my name in the *Guinness Book of World Records*.

I thought and thought, trying to figure out what I could get that would be the world's record. I even thought about it at dinner that night even though mealtime is when I usually concentrate on what I'm doing. I have to or my mom does sneaky things like hiding the peas under the mashed potatoes so I put them in my mouth without knowing it.

Hard telling what I consumed that night. For all I know, I may have eaten something really bad, like asparagus.

My mental effort paid off. After dinner, I sat on the back step with my dog, Jasper, and I took a piece of gum out of my pocket. unwrapped it, gave a little corner to Jasper, who swallowed it whole and then tried to separate the thin layer of tinfoil from the rest of the gum wrapper. I always do that with gum wrappers, to see if I can get the foil off in one piece.

I put my fingernail under one corner and carefully peeled back the foil. Then I rolled it into a little ball and held it in the palm of my hand. *That's how the shoe clerk got his start,* I thought. With a little rubber-band ball no bigger than my piece of foil.

And that's when I got my idea. I am going to have the world's greatest tinfoil collection. Starting with the piece of foil from my gum, I'll save every piece of foil I find. Foil doesn't break like rubber bands do, so there's no limit to the size of the ball I can make.

Only used tinfoil qualifies. Otherwise there wouldn't be any challenge. Anyone could buy boxes of foil and wad them up into a ball. My foil has to come from gum wrappers or packages of cigarettes or candy bars.

It isn't easy to become a world's record-holder. I spend a lot of time picking up litter on the streets and scrounging around in waste baskets. But it's worth it. My foil ball is almost two feet across already and getting bigger every day.

So watch for my name in the *Guinness Book of World Records* — and don't throw your gum wrappers away. Save 'em for me.

#59

Out-of-Body Choice

I hear you calling, Dad, but I don't want to come. Dad? Up here! Funny. He doesn't hear me at all, yet I can hear him as plain as anything. I can hear all of them down there, gathered around my body — Dad and Dr. Carson and the nurses. I can look down on them like I was looking at a movie, but even if they should look up, which doesn't seem likely, I know they wouldn't see me.

They think I'm still down there, lying on that hospital bed with my legs broken and my skull fractured. They didn't see me leave.

I don't feel any pain. I haven't, ever since I left my body behind. I felt myself drift up, ever so gently, up off the bed toward the ceiling. Above me, still farther up, there's a bright light, brighter than a dozen search lights, and it's where I want to go.

There are people there, beyond the light. I can't make out their faces, but I sense that they are kind people, loving people, and they want me to join them. They'll take care of me and help me. I'll be happy with them.

I want to float on now, to go into the light and join the others, but I'm held here, in limbo, just below the ceiling.

I know what holds me. It's Dad. The look on his face is terrible. The look of grief. I've seen it only once before — the day Mom died. I wonder if Mom looked down on us that day and saw our faces.

How can I do this to him? How can I allow myself to float on, into the happy light, knowing how he'll crumble?

I wish there was a way to tell him about the light and the happy people and the vibrations of love and peace. Then he wouldn't have that look on his face. Then he could smile.

Dad! I love you, Dad, but I'll be happier where I'm going. I'll be safe and . . . he's crying. Oh, God, my father is crying. For me. He's calling my name.

(Looks up and shields eyes, as if from bright light.) I wan
to come to you, kind people. Someday I will come, and gladly. Bu
right now . . . right now, I'm still needed down below. I hope you
understand. *(Drops hands; looks down.)*

I hear you, Dad. I hear you — and I'm coming.

#60

What Will I Be When I Grow Up?

People are always asking me what I want to be when I grow up, and I don't know how to answer. I can't imagine ever being grown-up. In my wildest dreams, I can't see myself being like my father and wearing a necktie and going off to work every morning. Going where? To what kind of work? I'm not at all sure I want to grow up and have a job.

Maybe I will be a veterinarian. I like cats and dogs a lot and I'm sure I'd like cows and horses, too, if I had a chance to know any. Veterinarians have to go to school a long time, though, and they have to do operations without getting sick themselves.

I'd like to be a mail carrier, too. Mail carriers get to go for long walks every day and say *hello* to the people on their route. I don't know if they have time to read all the postcards or not, but I know I'd want to. The only bad part is that they have to do their route even if it's snowing, and they sometimes get bit in the ankle.

It would be nice to own a Christmas tree farm. I could have acres and acres of green Christmas trees. In the summer, I'd water them and prune them, and in December, I'd sell them and then plant some more. But first I'd need to buy a lot of land, and where would I get the money for that?

Maybe I'll be a scientist and do research and discover the cure for a terrible disease. I'd get my picture on a postage stamp and have a vaccine named after me.

What I'd really like is to have more than one choice. I think I'll have a new career every ten years. When I'm in my twenties, I'll be a mail carrier because my legs will be strong and I'll like to walk. In my thirties, I'll be a veterinarian and save my money to buy some land so that in my forties I can have my Christmas tree farm. I'll be a scientist in my fifties, and in my sixties,

I'll probably be rich because of the cure I discovered, so I'll do something fun, like run a charter service for hot air balloon rides.

That's five different careers, and I think I'll like all of them. Maybe growing up won't be so bad, after all.

#61

Cotton Candy

I love cotton candy. I adore cotton candy. I know that sugar causes tooth decay and does all manner of terrible things to my body, but I still love cotton candy. It is easier to convince the mind than the tastebuds.

Over the years, I have experimented with various ways to eat cotton candy. All of them are fun and all of them make a mess. It is not possible to eat cotton candy daintily.

One way to eat cotton candy is to lean forward, put your face in the cotton candy, and take a bite. This method is extremely satisfying. For one thing, your nose will sink into the cotton candy right along with your mouth and the smell is absolutely wonderful. The problem with this method is that after only one bite, you will have a ring of sticky pink sugar all the way around your mouth and up on both cheeks. If you inhale too deeply, you'll have sugar in your nose, too, and quite likely there will be some sugar in your hair, as well.

Notice I say *pink* ring. Cotton candy does sometimes come in other colors, such as blue or white, but pink tastes the best. I always buy pink, no matter how many choices there are.

If you don't want to put your whole ace in the cotton candy, you can try to pull off little tufts, one at a time, and put them in your mouth. This method looks tidier, but the truth is, you will be every bit as much of a mess if you eat the cotton candy this way. Maybe even messier, because you'll now have the sticky sugar on your hand and you'll still get it all over your face, too, as you try to get the pieces in your mouth.

Even though you try to take teeny-weeny pieces, it isn't possible to do so. When you pull a piece of cotton candy off, it refuses to separate. It clings to itself, and even when you only pinch a small amount, more candy drifts after it, like the tail of a comet. You usually end up with a great wad which you have to stuff in your mouth.

If you lick your fingers to remove the excess cotton candy, you'll have sticky pink fingers, with little crystals of darker pink sugar here and there.

Once I tried eating cotton candy with a fork. I twisted the fork around in a circle, like you do with spaghetti. It worked pretty well except I twisted too long and couldn't get it all in my mouth in one piece and had to bite it off the fork in chunks. The big problem with this method is: who has a fork handy when they buy cotton candy?

No matter how sugary you are, never wipe your hands and face on a tissue. The cotton candy will not come off your skin onto the tissue, but the tissue will definitely come apart and stick to your skin. You'll not only have gooey pink sugar all over your hands and face, you'll also have little wisps of tissue stuck in the sugar.

You may be wondering why I go to so much trouble when popcorn, doughnuts and other easy-to-eat treats are plentiful. It's because cotton candy is light and fluffy and dissolves on my tongue without being chewed. It's like eating a cloud. A sweet, pink cloud. And if I'm a sticky mess when I'm done — well, it's worth it.

I love cotton candy.

#62

Auras

Mama wants me to pretend I don't see the colors. "You're makin' that up," she tells me. "There ain't no colors around people's heads."

"There are," I tell her, but she won't believe me.

"If everybody's got colors stickin' up out of their heads," she says, "why don't I see them?"

I can't answer that. I don't know why she can't see them. They're plain enough to me. There's pink around some people and yellow around others. Mrs. Mathews, who's my favorite teacher in the whole world, has a soft, gold color around her. Like sunshine on the autumn leaves. She's the one who told me what the colors are called. Auras. They're called auras, and she said I should be glad I can see the colors, that it's a special kind of gift.

Mama acts like it's more of a curse, something to be ashamed of. She gets real mad if I say anything about them when other people are around, and she makes me leave off the colors when I draw pictures of people. It's too bad, 'cause the pictures aren't half as pretty this way. I remember once I drew a picture of our family and I put the colors on everyone — pink and red around Mama, and a light yellow with flashes of brown around Daddy, and greens and blues around Sammy and Joe and Natalie. It was such a beautiful picture, with all those colors around everybody, like a rainbow. Mama didn't like it. She said I have an over-active imagination.

Once I saw a man with a black aura. I never saw a black one before and I've never seen one since, and I hope I never do again, either. It frightened me. He was standing by his car, and when I walked past him, he told me he had some candy for me and that I should get in his car and he'd give it to me. I didn't do it, though. I wanted the candy, but all that black color around his head scared me, so I just said I didn't want any and I ran for home.

Later, when I was old enough to go to school, Mama warned me never to get in a car with a stranger, but I didn't know that when I ran away from the man. All I knew was that I'd never seen black colors before and there was something threatening about it. I still get the willies, just remembering him, with all that black around him.

My grandma used to have a grey aura around her, a faint hazy grey. She lived with us for a time because she was too sickly to live alone. Mama used to get up in the night and give her the medicine. One day, I noticed that all the grey was gone. There wasn't any color around Grandma at all. When I told Mama about it, she said for me to hush up with my nonsense.

The next day, Grandma wasn't with us anymore. I wanted to ask if having the color disappear had anything to do with Grandma going to heaven, but Mama was already cryin' and feelin' so sad I didn't want to make her more upset by talking about Grandma's aura.

I don't know what color I have. I've stared and stared at myself in the mirror, but I never see any aura at all. Strange isn't it, when I can see the color around everyone else so nice and clear? Maybe nobody can ever see their own aura — or maybe just don't have one. For a time after Grandma died, I worried about it. I was afraid that since there wasn't any color around me, it meant I'd be going to heaven soon, too, and I don't want to go quite yet.

I don't worry anymore, because that was two years ago and I'm still here. I like to pretend that mine is gold, a soft, sunshiny gold, just like Mrs. Mathews'. But I don't tell Mama that.

#63

Student Sabbatical

My teacher, Mr. Maynard, is going to take a sabbatical leave next year. This means he won't be teaching for a whole year. Instead, he's going to travel to South America and study geology.

I think it's a fine idea. It would be even finer if students got to take a sabbatical. A whole year with no school! No piano lessons, either, and no club meetings and no chores. Just twelve long months to do whatever I want.

I've been thinking what I would do if I had an entire free year, a sabbatical leave of my own. First of all, I would lie in the grass more. Sometimes I would look down, and watch the ants or other little bugs that might be moving about. And sometimes I'd look up, and imagine pictures in the clouds. Sometimes I'd just lie with my eyes closed and listen to the wind in the leaves of the chestnut tree and inhale the sweet scent of grass and clover. With luck, the sun would shine down on my face and my little black dog would settle himself in the crook of my arm.

I also would learn to build rockets. Model rockets out of balsa wood and glue. I'd make basic rockets and complicated rockets and rockets with designs painted on their sides. I'd take my fleet of rockets out to a big open field and I'd shoot them off and watch them go high up in the sky, and then I'd run across the field and try to find them again when they landed.

I would read the encyclopedia. All of it, from *Aardvark* to *Zucchini*. Every time I look something up in the encyclopedia, I get sidetracked and read all about whatever is listed before and after the thing I started to look up. Then I run out of time and have to leave the library before I'm finished. If I had a sabbatical, I could read the encyclopedia all day long, until I was finished.

Maybe I would also learn to cook. Yes. I'd learn to make all my favorite foods — spaghetti and pizza and chocolate cream pie — and then I could have them any time I wanted.

Mr. Maynard says the purpose of a sabbatical leave is to refresh the spirit and challenge the intellect by a complete change in daily routine. He says at the end of the sabbatical, he will want to come back and teach again.

I think my spirit would be refreshed and my intellect would be challenged if I could spend a whole year building rockets and reading the encyclopedia and lying in the grass and making chocolate cream pie. I'm not so sure, though, about wanting to come back to school and piano lessons and chores at the end of the year. I rather think I'd want the sabbatical to continue, to go on, month after month and year after year.

Maybe that's why the teachers get to have sabbaticals and not the students. We can't be trusted to return.

#64

Merry Birthday

I was born on December twenty-fifth. Can you imagine such poor planning on the part of my parents? I don't think there's a worse time to have a birthday.

No one gets excited about my birthday except me. Everyone is opening the little doors on Advent calendars and wrapping presents and baking red and green cookies. My birthday always gets overlooked.

Even worse, I get what people call "joint" Christmas-birthday presents. That means since I had the misfortune to be born on December twenty-fifth, I only get one present each year instead of two. I have never quite understood the reasoning behind this. If my birthday came in April, everyone would give me a birthday present in April and a Christmas present in December. It seems logical to me that since my birthday is in December, I should get a birthday present in December and a Christmas present in December. That isn't how it works, though. I get one present and it has to do double duty.

All my friends have parties on their birthdays. I have never once had a party on my birthday because at least half of the people I would want to invite are celebrating Christmas with their families that day. *I'm* celebrating Christmas with my family that day and there's no way we could handle a birthday party at the same time.

I don't even get a birthday cake. Plum pudding on Christmas has been traditional in my dad's family for generations and Mom always makes her special fudge and peanut brittle. To be honest, I'd rather have plum pudding and fudge and peanut brittle than a piece of cake, but I can't help feeling cheated.

One time I had a half-year birthday party, on June twenty-fifth. All my friends came and we had a birthday cake and played games. I got lots of presents that year, but it still wasn't the same. I knew it wasn't really my birthday and so did everyone else. The party seemed like a pretend party, not a real one.

My uncle told me that Christmas isn't really on December twenty-fifth. He said that's just the traditional date to celebrate it in our culture. I've thought a lot about that. I even considered writing to Congress and suggesting we change Christmas to some other day, but I decided it wouldn't do any good. How would they ever decide which day to change it to?

I can't change my birthday, either. I could go to court and legally change my name, but I'm stuck with my birthday forever.

I wish that some year, just once, everyone would forget about Christmas. Forget about trimming a tree and making fudge. Sing only "Happy Birthday" instead of "Joy to the World." Forget the plum pudding and the . . . wait a minute. That would be terrible! No Christmas carols? No Santa? We *can't* forget Christmas. I guess I'll just have my birthday on December twenty-fifth, as usual. Maybe this year I'll eat two pieces of plum pudding.

#65

The Winner

There was a competition at our school last year. A poetry competition. Anyone who wanted to could write a poem and enter it in the contest. The best ten were printed in a booklet and the first-prize winner received twenty-five dollars and a framed certificate.

I wanted to win that contest more than I ever wanted anything in my life. Not for the twenty-five dollars, although I could have used the money. I wanted to win because deep down inside me I wanted to be a writer and I wasn't sure if I had any talent. I thought if I won first prize in a poetry competition, it would mean I do have some ability.

I'm not real good at most other things. Especially sports. Everyone else jogs and works out. They lift weights and play tennis or volleyball. I hate exercising. I'm always the last one to be chosen when we pick teams for baseball or basketball. And the only reason I passed Physical Education last year was because my gym partner lied for me and said I'd done the required three push-ups when I could barely manage one.

Maybe that's why the poetry contest was so important to me. When you're really rotten at most things, you want to be extra-good at the few things you care about.

I worked on my contest entry every day for two weeks. I wrote seven different poems and threw all of them away. I wrote about butterflies and kittens and the way I feel when I hear certain kinds of music. None of my poems was any good. I crumpled them up and threw them in my wastebasket. I wanted them to be beautiful, and instead, they were awkward and crude.

But I didn't give up. I kept writing. I revised and changed the words around and thought up new ideas for poems.

And then, on the last night before the contest deadline, I wrote a poem that I knew was good. It was a simple poem, but every time I read it, I got goosebumps on my arms. I knew it was the best writing I'd ever done. I called it "Unicorn Magic" and I entered it in the contest the next morning.

The winner was not announced until two weeks later. During those two weeks, I floated in a special dream, imagining how it would be to sit at the awards program in the school auditorium and hear my name announced as the first-prize winner in the poetry competiton.

On the day of the awards, I couldn't eat breakfast. I wore my new grey pants, the ones that make me look thinner than I am. I got up half an hour early so I'd have time to wash my hair.

Before the winner was announced, the principal read the names of the authors of the ten best poems. Mine was one of them. My heart began to pound and my mouth got all dry. Then he announced the winner: first prize to Kathy Enderson for her poem titled "Goldfish Jubilee."

When Kathy's name was called, she shrieked and jumped up and all her friends screamed and cheered. I just sat there, stunned. I couldn't believe "Unicorn Magic" had lost when it made me get goosebumps every time I read it. Maybe I wasn't going to be a writer, after all. Maybe I had no talent. If Kathy Enderson, who laughs at dirty jokes and flirts with all the guys and thinks being a cheerleader is the most important thing in the world, if Kathy can write better poetry than I can, then I might as well give it up forever.

Except I couldn't. I went home that day and wrote a poem about how much it hurt to lose the competition. When I read the poem again the next morning, I got goosebumps on my arms and I knew I would keep on writing, even if I never won any awards.

I studied Kathy's poem in the booklet. I had to admit it was good.

That summer, long after the poetry competition was over and school was out, I was looking through some magazines in the public library and I came across a poem titled "Goldfish Jubilee."

'or one awful moment, I thought Kathy had not only won the contest, he'd actually had her poem published. Then I saw the author's ame. Andrew Billings. "Goldfish Jubilee" by Andrew Billings. he poem was the same; the author was not.

I looked at the date on the magazine. It was published a nonth before our poetry competition.

Should I show it to the principal and demand that the poems e judged again? Should I call Kathy Enderson and tell her I knew he'd cheated? What good would it do? That special moment in he school auditorium, when the winner's name was announced, as over. It was too late.

I hate Kathy Enderson for what she did, but I feel sorry or her, too. She has a certificate that says *First Prize, Poetry 'ompetition,* and she has the twenty-five dollars, but she doesn't now how it feels to read her very own poem and get goosebumps n her arms.

And she'll never know.

ABOUT THE AUTHOR

Peg Kehret enjoys a dual profession: playwright and novelist. Her funny, heart-warming plays have been produced in all 50 states and Canada, while her books for young people have earned a wide readership and critical acclaim.

Early in her career, Peg wrote radio commercials. Later, she published magazine fiction, articles, light verse, educational scripts and adult nonfiction books.

Among her many honors are the Forest Roberts Playwriting Award, a Children's Choice Award, the Pacific Northwest Writer's Conference Achievement Award, the Young Hoosier Book Award (nominated by Indiana school children), and selection by the American Library Association for its Recommended Books for Reluctant Readers. Her books are frequently on Young Reader's Choice lists for various states and her work has been published in Denmark, Australia, Norway, Portugal, Canada, and Scotland.

Peg and her husband, Carl, live in Washington State. They have two grown children and four grandchildren.

ALSO BY PEG KEHRET

Books for Young People:

Acting Natural

**Encore! More Winning Monologs
for Young Actors**

Adult Books:

Wedding Vows

Order Form

Meriwether Publishing Ltd.
P.O. Box 7710
Colorado Springs, CO 80933
Telephone: (719) 594-4422 Fax: (719) 594-9916

Please send me the following books:

_____ **Winning Monologs for Young Actors**   **$14.95**
#BK-B127
by Peg Kehret
Honest-to-life monologs for young actors

_____ **Encore! More Winning Monologs for**   **$14.95**
Young Actors #BK-B144
by Peg Kehret
More honest-to-life monologs for young actors

_____ **Acting Natural #BK-B133**   **$14.95**
by Peg Kehret
Honest-to-life monologs, dialogs and playlets for teens

_____ **Theatre Games for Young Performers**   **$14.95**
#BK-B188
by Maria C. Novelly
Improvisations and exercises for developing acting skills

_____ **Spotlight #BK-B176**   **$12.95**
by Stephanie S. Fairbanks
Solo scenes for student actors

_____ **Wedding Vows #BK-B151**   **$11.95**
by Peg Kehret
How to express your love in your own words

_____ **The Flip Side #BK-B221**   **$12.95**
by Heather H. Henderson
64 point-of-view monologs for teens

**These and other fine Meriwether Publishing books are available at
your local bookstore or direct from the publisher. Use the handy
order form on this page.**

Name: _____

Organization name: _____

Address: _____

City: _____ State: _____

Zip: _____ Phone: _____

❏ **Check Enclosed**
❏ **Visa or MasterCard #** _____

Expiration
Signature: _____ *Date:* _____

(required for Visa/MasterCard orders)

COLORADO RESIDENTS: Please add 3% sales tax.
SHIPPING: Include $2.75 for the first book and 50¢ for each additional book ordered.

❏ *Please send me a copy of your complete catalog of books and plays*